Everyday Wild is an illustrated celebration of the vast natural diversity of the world, one that you can find by simply stepping outside. This guide to backyard (or front stoop!) ecology encourages you to notice every sight, sound, and smell—the rustle of falling leaves, the chirping of crickets, the scent of spring rain, and the radiance of the stars above—as a way of understanding the wonders of our complex, beautiful planet.

EVERYDAY
WILD

EVERYDAY WILD

An Illustrated Guide for
Mindfulness in Nature

KATHRYN HUNTER AND BO HUNTER

Clarkson Potter/Publishers

New York, New York

CONTENTS

AT SOME POINT IN LIFE
THE WORLD'S BEAUTY
BECOMES ENOUGH.
YOU DON'T NEED TO
PHOTOGRAPH, PAINT, OR
EVEN REMEMBER IT.
IT IS ENOUGH.

-TONI MORRISON, TAR BABY

Introduction

KATHRYN AND I GREW UP IN DECATUR, ALABAMA, on the Tennessee River. We share a sense of adventure that comes from our sibling adventures into the woods and backwaters of North Alabama. The summer after my freshman year of college, I took a job that indelibly changed my relationship to nature. I was one of the first employees to arrive at Yellowstone National Park for the season in late May, and the snow still covered much of the park. My connection to this truly magical piece of landscape was immediate.

I remember writing a postcard to Kathryn after only a week, telling her about the cow, a female moose, I just witnessed giving birth to her calf—right under my nose. I had never even seen a moose before that day. I climbed onto the roof of a cabin with two coworkers to observe the miracle. For the rest of the summer, I would continue to watch the mama nudge and help her calf grow as they stayed near the cabin where the calf was born.

Steamboat Geyser, the world's tallest currently active geyser, went off under a full moon only a few weeks later. My friends and I drove fifteen miles following the geyser's steam as it rose hundreds of feet into the night sky, billowing under a big Yellowstone moon. You can't help but feel connected to the planet in moments like those. Yellowstone is all about the activity of living and dying, all day every day. As far as Kathryn and I are concerned, it is the most sacred place on the planet.

Kathryn followed suit two years later, when she spent her first summer in Yellowstone. She had a similar experience, only the ancient pull of Yellowstone wouldn't release her, so she spent almost ten years in the area. Kathryn's art will always nod to the natural world around us; her heart will always be in the highlands.

When we both returned to the south—me to Tennessee and my sister to Louisiana—we were changed. Only then did we truly begin to fully appreciate the brilliance and beauty of the natural world that surrounded us in new homes as well as in our birth state of Alabama—but also everywhere we went! That ancient call to get outdoors hasn't weakened. In fact, as we've gotten older, we've found it more important than ever. The great outdoors is the only place to recharge and rekindle a sense of well-being. It is a reliable place to pause and be present in our bodies and minds. It is also an evergreen classroom, a place to learn about science and the laws of nature at work all around us. Nature's beauty often goes unnoticed in our daily lives, in turn depriving us of a sense of wonder and the profound connection to the earth that our lives depend on. Has your FOMO ratcheted up yet?

Kathryn's interest in Buddhist traditions—which relate so much to our interconnectedness with the earth and each other—and my deep-rooted fascination with philosophy—especially the Eastern traditions—have informed a lot of the content in the following pages. While we both believe in the positive power of transcendental meditation, we both find that everyday moments of mindfulness are easily accessible and something to be pursued as we navigate this busy world we all live in.

Kathryn and I have collaborated in spirit in so many ways to form our worldviews, learning from and with each other throughout our lives. Our collaboration on this book has been an exciting act of uncovering the opportunities for wonder found just beyond your front step. We hope this book gives your mind a place to take a beat to contemplate the grandeur of the natural world and piques your curiosity. Nature is our ever dependable access point to mindfulness. Enjoy the wonderful illustrations and lessons in these pages, then go outside and just *be* with your wonderful world.

YELLOW GARDEN SPIDER
3", BODY ¾" to 1"

MOST OF US WALK UNSEEING THROUGH
THE WORLD, UNAWARE ALIKE OF ITS
BEAUTIES, ITS WONDERS, AND THE STRANGE
AND SOMETIMES TERRIBLE INTENSITY OF
THE LIVES THAT ARE BEING LIVED ABOUT US.

—RACHEL CARSON, SILENT SPRING

CHAPTER 1

NOTICE THE SMALL THINGS

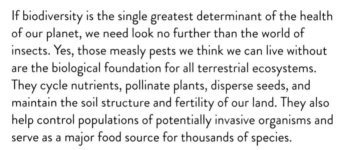

If biodiversity is the single greatest determinant of the health of our planet, we need look no further than the world of insects. Yes, those measly pests we think we can live without are the biological foundation for all terrestrial ecosystems. They cycle nutrients, pollinate plants, disperse seeds, and maintain the soil structure and fertility of our land. They also help control populations of potentially invasive organisms and serve as a major food source for thousands of species.

It is here, in the world of insects, where we can see fifty million years of cooperation and technologies that have enabled our planet to survive. We don't have to love insects, but if in a mindful moment we offer them our attention, we can experience the awe of watching them do their work, witness their social contracts with one another, and—on a small scale— see the cooperation of all living things.

As you read this, there are somewhere around 10 quadrillion ants on earth, each performing a specific job for the greater good of our planet.

SOME INSECTS

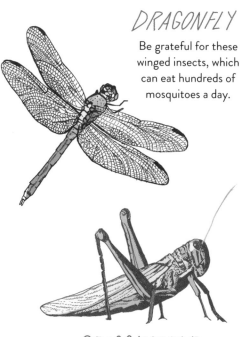

DRAGONFLY

Be grateful for these winged insects, which can eat hundreds of mosquitoes a day.

All insects have a head, thorax, abdomen, antenna, and six jointed legs.

JUNEBUG

These plant-eating beetles have been around since before the dinosaurs!

GRASSHOPPER

These nitrogen-rich insects facilitate plant decomposition and growth. When they die, the soil easily breaks down their bodies, which infuses it with nitrogen. They also prevent plant overgrowth by feeding on vegetation.

While a certain four Beatles will always be the most fabulous, beetles make up 40 percent of all insect species, with more than 380,000 species described to date.

WASP

Besides being pollinators, wasps cull overpopulations of other insects like beetles, spiders, and caterpillars by taking them to feed their young.

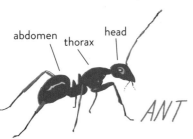

abdomen thorax head

ANT

These complex insects aerate the soil, allowing water and oxygen to get to plants' roots.

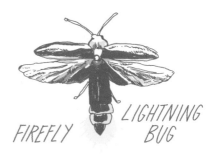

FIREFLY   **LIGHTNING BUG**

These neon-blinking flying beetles light up to attract a mate.

HONEY BEE

The ultimate pollinators, honey bees pollinate 80 percent of the world's plants.

BOXELDER BUG

Also called box bugs and maple bugs, boxelder bugs suck on the leaves and seeds of boxelder and maple trees to pull sugar from them to eat without actually hurting the trees.

MOSQUITO

These nippers are also pollinators, transferring pollen from flower to flower as they feed on nectar. Did you know that only the female mosquito seeks a blood meal and only when she lays her eggs?

HOUSEFLY

These pesky little pests clean up our mess by eating decomposing garbage, food, and animal dung.

COMMON SPIDERS

Many of us have a hardwired instinct to squash insects and spiders or call pest control when we see a few bugs. Before acting on this impulse, be mindful that spiders are considered "beneficial predators." They make feasts out of many household pests that can transmit disease to humans. They enjoy dining on mosquitoes, fleas, flies, cockroaches, and a multitude of other disease-carrying critters.

ARROWHEAD

< 1/4 "

SPIRAL ORB WEB

MARBLED ORB WEAVER 3/4"

TRIANGLE WEB

TRIANGLE WEAVER
$< ^3/_8"$

HOBO $^1/_4" - ^5/_8"$

FUNNEL WEB

Fun fact:
A spider dangling from its web was seen as a sign of good luck in ancient Chinese culture.

DADDY LONGLEGS A.K.A. HARVESTMEN

body ⁵/₁₆"
legspan 6"

True or false?
Daddy longlegs have
the deadliest venom and
could kill humans if their
fangs were larger.

False! Daddy longlegs
have no venom at all.
They are not even
considered spiders
(and do not make webs),
though they are in the
same class, Arachnida.

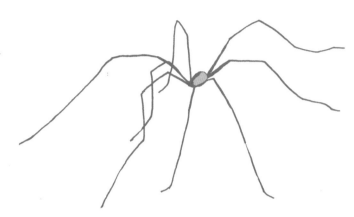

WOLF
½" - 2"

*spins no web, but instead
creates burrows*

JUMPING
⅛" - ⅞"

*makes a web for resting
and not for catching prey*

BOWL AND DOILY
⅛"

makes a sheet web

DID YOU KNOW

... that no two spiderwebs are the same? If you are lucky enough to witness a spider weaving its web, you are observing a genius at work. Pause and take in this sacred act of creation.

THESE SPIDERS MAKE A TANGLED WEB

AMERICAN HOUSE < 1/4 "

BLACK WIDOW
1 1/2 " POISONOUS

BROWN RECLUSE
about 1" POISONOUS

MOTHS

Moth caterpillars love to eat the foliage of trees like birch, ash, poplar, hickory, sweet gum, and plum.

Many adult moths, like the luna and the cecropia, do not eat at all, and their only purpose is to reproduce in their short lifespan of one to two weeks. But others, like the twin-spotted sphinx, drink nectar from long-throated flowers, similar to hummingbirds.

LUNA
3" – 4½"

FALL WEBWORM
1¼" – 1½"

POLYPHEMUS
4" – 6"

BROWN HOUSE
½" to 1"

TWIN-SPOTTED SPHINX
1¾" – 3¼"

IO
2" – 3⅛"

The cecropia caterpillar grows up to four inches long and eats voraciously for a few weeks before spinning a cocoon. When the cecropia becomes a moth, it stops eating and focuses solely on mating.

CECROPIA 5" – 7"

BUTTERFLIES

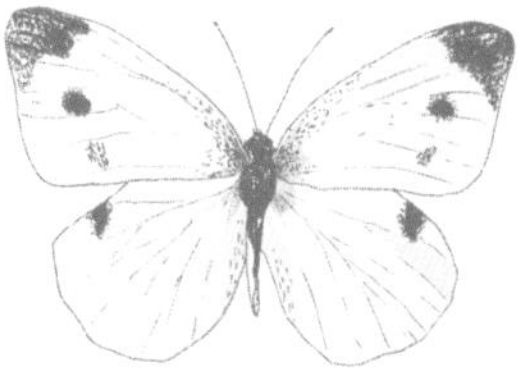

CABBAGE WHITE
1¼" - 1⅞"

PIPELINE SWALLOWTAIL
2¾" - 5⅛"

CLOUDLESS SULPHUR
2" - 3"

MALACHITE
2¾" - 3¼"

BLACK SWALLOWTAIL
2¾" - 3¼"

To attract butterflies, plant: purple coneflower, aster, lantana, zinnias, phlox, cosmos, angelica, yarrow, Mexican sunflower, and snapdragon.

To feed caterpillars, plant: parsley (for black swallowtail), nettle and hops (for red admiral), cabbage and Brussels sprouts (for cabbage white), thistle (for American painted lady), and common milkweed (for monarch).

RED ADMIRAL
1¾" - 3"

AMERICAN PAINTED LADY
2" - 2⅞"

MONARCH

3"-4"

Butterflies are the ultimate reminder to trust the process, and that life is a series of physical phases, each challenging us to grow and accept change with patience. Some phases come and go quickly, while others last much longer. The butterfly begins as an egg and within three or four days becomes a caterpillar (larva). The two weeks that it lives as a caterpillar, it experiences rapid growth.

In this eating and growing phase, the caterpillar will shed its skin four times or more to keep up with its rapidly growing body. The caterpillar's time in its chrysalis might seem like a dormant period in its life, but it is going through big changes, and its metamorphosis into the adult butterfly is imminent.

Monarch butterflies are the great wayfaring strangers, traveling up to three thousand miles on their two-way migration from Mexico to Canada each year. The monarch butterfly's annual flight to Mexico coincides with the Día de los Muertos (Day of the Dead). The Purépecha, Indigenous people in northwestern Mexico, have tracked the insect's return to Mexico for centuries. The perennial homecoming of the butterflies, known as La Parakata, also signifies the time for the corn harvest. The Parakatas were believed to be the souls of the dead visiting for the celebration of the deceased. The return of the monarch continues to have strong cultural meaning for Mexicans even today, representing the connection between the living and the dead.

MONARCH LIFE CYCLE

EGG

CATERPILLAR

CHRYSALIS

ADULT
BUTTERFLY

*POLLINATING
ECHINACEA PURPUREA*

Monarch caterpillars thrive by eating milkweed.
To attract them, grow common milkweed in your yard (avoid
planting tropical milkweed), either in the ground or in a pot.

REFLECTION:
THE BUTTERFLY EFFECT

The butterfly effect in chaos theory, proposed by Edward Lorenz in 1961, is the phenomenon whereby a minute, localized change in a complex system can have a large effect elsewhere. It directly opposed Isaac Newton's tidy, predictable "clockwork universe," which relied on predictability. Lorenz's idea was that something small or random, even imperceptible, can change things dramatically. His prime example was that the energy created by a butterfly beating its wings in Rio de Janeiro could theoretically be a catalyst that generates a tornado in Chicago. Lorenz would later write that there was an equal likelihood that the energy created by the butterfly's wings could have the exact opposite effect by *preventing* a tornado from forming—these unpredictable outcomes from the same initial action defined the chaos theory.

ROBIN

THE WHOLE IS NECESSARILY EVERYTHING.
THE WHOLE WORLD OF FACT AND FANCY, BODY
AND PSYCHE, PHYSICAL FACT AND SPIRITUAL
TRUTH, INDIVIDUAL AND COLLECTIVE, LIFE
AND DEATH, MACROCOSM AND MICROCOSM...
CONSCIOUS AND UNCONSCIOUS, SUBJECT
AND OBJECT. THE WHOLE PICTURE IS
PORTRAYED BY IS, THE DEEPEST WORD
OF ULTIMATE REALITY...

-JOHN STEINBECK, THE LOG FROM THE SEA OF CORTEZ

CHAPTER 2

CONNECT THE DOTS

A Declaration of Interdependence. Interconnectedness and deep reciprocity create the foundation of all living things. There are no big and small gestures in nature . . . because everything is connected. The closer you look, the more you will find that everything is special and intentional—nothing is common or mundane. Every aspect of nature is necessary to the life cycle of some living thing's birth, life, and death. Everything in nature interacts in a purposeful way for the survival of the planet. Pay attention and find joy in this co-dependence and connection as you witness the bee pollinating a plant or the summer breeze carrying a wintered-over seed to a more fertile plane. The food we eat, every breath we take, every step we make, sets these interactions in motion.

HOW POLLINATION WORKS

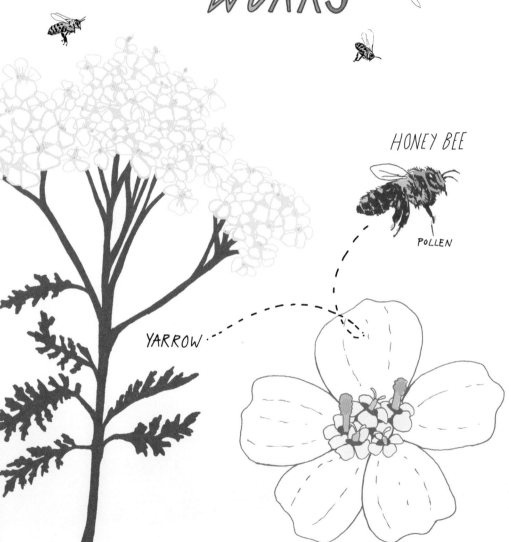

HONEY BEE

POLLEN

YARROW

Bee excited! When a bee lands on a flower, here is what happens: The pollen from the male reproductive organ of the flower sticks to the hairs of the bee's body. When the bee flies off and lands on another flower for more sustenance, the sac of pollen falls off the bee and spills over to the new flower. So as the bee flits to another flower, the cycle begins again, and the lives of the bees and the flowers continue their waltz.

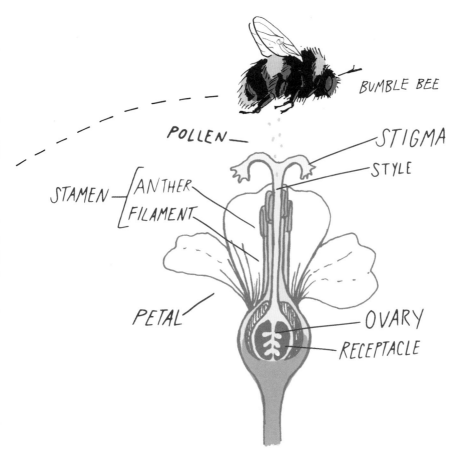

BUMBLE BEE

POLLEN

STIGMA

STYLE

STAMEN — { ANTHER
{ FILAMENT

PETAL

OVARY

RECEPTACLE

FOOD THAT NEEDS POLLINATION

When you see a bee land on a flower, rejoice, because life on earth would not be sustainable without pollination. Humanity and all of earth's terrestrial ecosystems depend on pollinators to move across the planet spreading pollen.

GARLIC-
BEES, BUTTERFL
MOTHS

EGGPLANT-
BUMBLEBEES

BRUSSELS SPROUTS-
HONEYBEES AND
NATIVE BEES

WATERMELON-
NATIVE BEES

PARSLEY-
HOVERFLIES

Why? Because 80 percent of all crops that provide us with food and plant-based products require pollination to grow, bloom, and fruit. The pollinator team is a motley crew that includes ants, bats, birds, beetles, butterflies, flies, moths, and wasps.

PHOTOSYNTHESIS

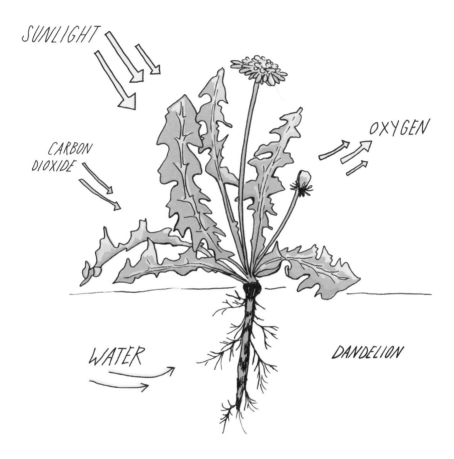

SUNLIGHT

CARBON
DIOXIDE

OXYGEN

WATER

DANDELION

Photosynthesis is the harmonious exchange between oxygen-breathers and carbon-eaters. Leaves and stems of plants where the energy of the sun is stored contain chlorophyll, which makes them green. The healthy green plant then consumes the carbon dioxide, or CO_2, in the atmosphere. Humans breathe in oxygen and breathe out carbon dioxide; plants breathe in CO_2 and breathe out oxygen. Thus, the cycle of reciprocity continues. Perhaps talking to your plants is not as crazy as it seems.

LEAF CROSS-SECTION

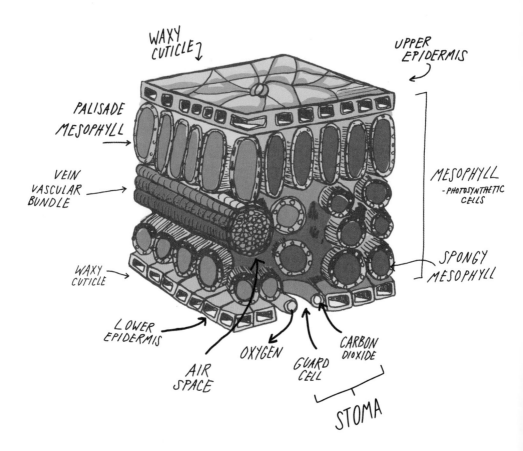

WAXY CUTICLE

UPPER EPIDERMIS

PALISADE MESOPHYLL

VEIN VASCULAR BUNDLE

MESOPHYLL - PHOTOSYNTHETIC CELLS

SPONGY MESOPHYLL

WAXY CUTICLE

LOWER EPIDERMIS

OXYGEN

CARBON DIOXIDE

AIR SPACE

GUARD CELL

STOMA

Leaves are the most important organs of most vascular plants. They manufacture food by sucking up water and minerals from their roots and absorbing CO_2 from the air. Then leaves convert these ingredients into food by using the energy from the sun, which ultimately helps nourish and sustain all land animals.

PALISADE MESOPHYLL

most of photosynthesis happens in this layer due to the high number of chloroblasts in each cell, which produce energy during the process

VEIN VASCULAR BUNDLE

the part of the system that transports water and food through the leaf

GUARD CELLS

opens or closes the stomata controlling water loss in the leaf

SPONGY MESOPHYLL

helps the exchange of oxygen and carbon dioxide during photosynthesis

STOMA

opening for gas exchange

MYCORRHIZAL NETWORKS

Scientists are beginning to learn how trees communicate between one another and with other vegetation. Trees are not lone rangers depriving other trees of resources to grow and thrive, as natural selection might suggest. On the contrary, evidence suggests that trees have evolved to live cooperatively with trees of the same species in their neighborhoods. They converse through intricate underground webs called mycorrhizal networks. They use this network, often nicknamed the Wood Wide Web, to share water and nutrients and send distress signals about drought and disease in their vicinity.

PINE TREE

Old-growth "mother trees," while not always female, are the biggest and oldest trees in the forest and have the most fungal connections below the surface. They have an outsize impact on the overall health of a forest.

LITTER-DEGRADING SAPROTROPHIC FUNGI

MYCELIUM

CARBON →

SUGAR →

SYMBIOTIC FUNGAL NETWORK

The mycorrhizal network is a web of fine, hairline root tips joined together with microscopic fungal filaments, an underground communication system that supports the transmission of chemical, hormonal, and electric signals among plants of all kinds. Trees will sometimes adopt plants of other species to ensure the overall health of their neighbors, by rejecting sugars and minerals and transferring them back to the soil through their roots, which in turn benefits the entire ecosystem's overall health.

BIRCH TREE (MOTHER TREE)

DISTRESS SIGNALS

MYCELIUM

WATER + NUTRIENTS

CARBON

SUGAR

WHY IS A TREE IMPORTANT?

Life on our planet doesn't exist without trees. Trees help produce the rain, clean the rivers, store carbon, and provide oxygen, all while harboring much of the biodiversity of the planet.

Even though most people don't move to cities for the trees, they offer great value in urban environments. Their leaves absorb pollution particulates, protecting us from breathing in toxins. They slow storm water and stave off flooding. And in a very practical way, city trees cool the concrete jungle and provide shade on scorching days. As of 2020, the City of New York Parks and Recreation research suggests trees save the city approximately $27 million a year on cooling costs.

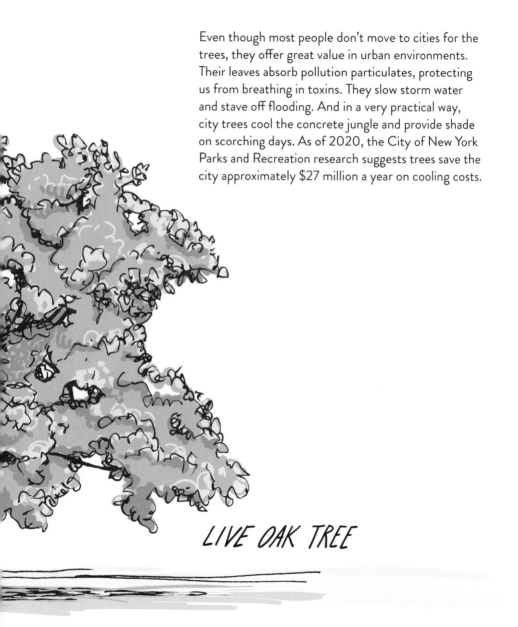

LIVE OAK TREE

**Birds and small animals like raccoons depend on trees
for shelter, food, mating, and hunting.**

Trees also benefit from the birds they harbor. Some birds, like the pileated woodpecker, chickadee, red-eyed vireo, and nuthatch feed on insects, like beetles and mites that damage trees, and help keep non-threatening insects to a healthy number. They also disperse seeds from their diet as they defecate (sometimes in flight!) and move saplings and other plant life to further the biodiversity of the woods.

*PILEATED
WOODPECKERS
BUILD A
CAVITY NEST*

*AND SO DO
RACCOONS!*

THESE BIRDS MAKE A CUP NEST

RED-EYED VIREO

RED-EYED VIREO NEST

NUTHATCH

CHICKADEE

A NUTHATCH OFTEN MAKES A CUP NEST INSIDE A CAVITY!

FUN FACT:
CHICKADEES CAN EAT UP TO A THOUSAND INSECTS A DAY!

ACTION: PLANT A SUNFLOWER

To plant a seed is to hope; to have faith that you will live to see it blossom, that it might benefit you personally and everything around it as it grows. Delight in the simplicity of planting a seed and imagining the life it will live as it grows.

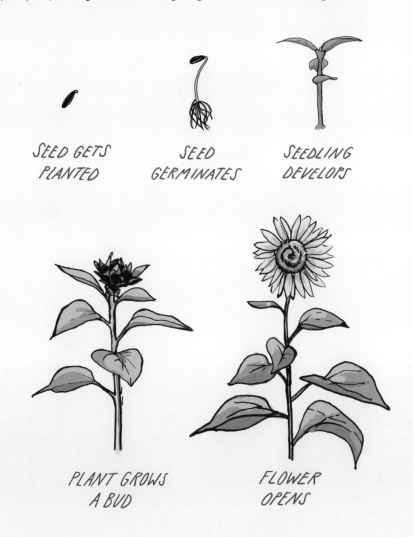

SEED GETS
PLANTED

SEED
GERMINATES

SEEDLING
DEVELOPS

PLANT GROWS
A BUD

FLOWER
OPENS

SEEDS DEVELOP
SEEDS RIPEN AND DRY

PLANT DROPS SEEDS
COLLECT SEEDS AND
PLANT AGAIN

OYSTER
MUSHROOMS

THE PURPOSE OF LIFE,
AFTER ALL, IS TO LIVE IT,
TO TASTE EXPERIENCE TO
THE UTMOST, TO REACH OUT
EAGERLY AND WITHOUT FEAR
FOR NEWER AND RICHER
EXPERIENCE.
-ELEANOR ROOSEVELT

HICKORY TREE

CHAPTER 3

TASTE THE WILD

Foraging offers us a great reason to get out
into the natural world. It is an immersive way
to learn a plant's life cycle, find balanced ways
of harvesting sustainably, and satisfy culinary
curiosity. Foraging helps us understand where
our food comes from and connects us with
our most primitive selves. The land we forage
becomes a very specific classroom where we
engage all our senses.

SAFETY FIRST! *INDENTIFYING POISONOUS PLANTS*

Note that NOT all nuts, berries, flowers, and mushrooms are safe for human consumption. In fact, some are poisonous. It is not only advisable but necessary to learn from a mentor and use well-researched guidebooks to help you identify wild plants to eat. By doing so, you will get to know the plants in your area by observing, touching, and smelling them, and by educating yourself about edible plant life. Then, when you find what you are looking for, enjoy their wild deliciousness. The single most important aspect of foraging is accurately identifying healthy versus dangerous plants.

Some common poisonous plants to look out for:

STINGING NETTLES

can cause a painful rash on skin contact.

WILD PARSNIP

intensifies sun exposure when it touches the skin and will generate severe sunburn within twenty-four to forty-eight hours. It looks like Queen Anne's lace (or wild carrot) but has yellow flowers. While the roots are edible, all the other parts are poisonous.

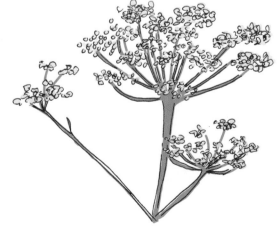

POISON IVY

POISON OAK

POISON SUMAC

Poison oak, poison ivy, and poison sumac all contain the chemical urushiol, which causes an allergic reaction on the skin, usually an itchy rash that will turn into blisters.

FLY AGARIC, AMANITA MUSCARIA

Fly agaric or *Amanita muscaria* is a mushroom that's poisonous if ingested but not deadly. It causes unpredictable symptoms, ranging from nausea, headaches, dizziness, and delirium to seizures in extreme cases.

 DO NOT EAT ANYTHING YOU CANNOT 100% IDENTIFY

LOOK FOR THESE EDIBLE WILD FRUITS
(HARVESTING TIME WILL DEPEND ON THE REGION)

PAWPAW

AKA custard apple, is the largest edible fruit in North America. Its habitat is the eastern US.

BLACKBERRIES

are packed full of vitamin C and fiber. The best news is that they have no poisonous look-alikes. They are easy to identify, and the only berries that might be mistaken for them are the equally delicious black raspberries. They are found throughout the US.

ROSEHIPS

make a great-tasting tea that may remind you of tart strawberries. To make it, you can use either fresh or dried bulbs. Rosehips are super high in vitamin C. They can be harvested from wild rose bushes after the first frost in fall and can be found throughout the US.

WILD STRAWBERRIES

dangle on the vine and have white or pink flowers and they taste sweet, while mock strawberries taste bland (but are not poisonous). They have yellow flowers and the fruit grows on top of the plant. You can find both throughout the US.

PRICKLY PEAR

tastes like melon and can be harvested when fully red, with no green remaining. You can find this drought-tolerant plant in warm, dry parts of the western US.

SOME EDIBLE NUTS TO HARVEST IN THE FALL

Foraging for nuts, also known as nutting, is very easily done once you have identified a tree and learned what season its fruit ripens, which is most often in the fall. Nuts are full of protein and fat.

HAZELNUTS that are native to North America are found in Canada, and the East, Southeast, and Midwest of the US. The California hazelnut grows in forests along the Pacific coast from British Columbia to California. Pick an entire cluster and let them dry. Crack the shells with a nutcracker.

PECANS are found throughout the US. Once you learn to identify the pecan tree, you may spot them on a walk through the city or perhaps in your own yard. In the fall, nuts drop from the tree when ripened and are easily cracked with a nutcracker. Their delicious meat can be eaten raw or roasted.

PINE NUTS come from the pinyon pine in the western US. In late summer or early fall, following several dry days, lay a blanket or tarp under the tree and shake it until the nuts fall.

Black walnuts and hickory nuts are hard nuts to crack. You'll need a hammer to get to the small but delicious meat inside them. Black walnuts are found in the eastern half of the US; Arizona and California black walnuts are found in the western US. Hickory nuts are found in the eastern and central US.

BLACK WALNUT

HICKORY

EDIBLE FLOWERS FOUND FROM SPRING TO LATE SUMMER THROUGHOUT THE U.S.

Many flowers are edible, delicious, and nutritious! Those determined little dandelions that keep creeping up in your yard are included in this group. But don't eat them if you use fertilizer and pesticides. The flowers can be eaten raw or tossed in a salad. The roots can be steeped in hot water to make tea.

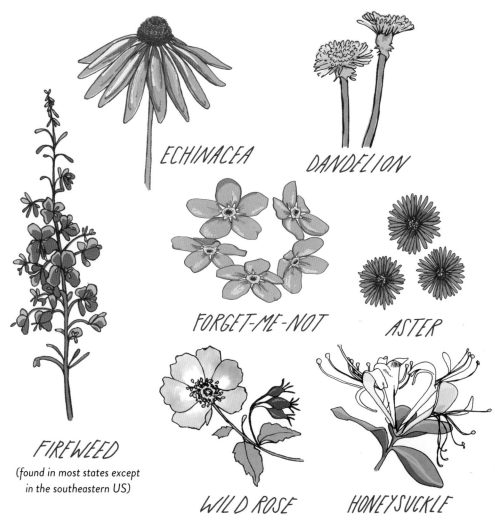

ECHINACEA

DANDELION

FORGET-ME-NOT

ASTER

FIREWEED
(found in most states except in the southeastern US)

WILD ROSE

HONEYSUCKLE

WILD GREENS FOUND THROUGHOUT THE U.S. IN SPRING

WILD LETTUCE

Finding delicious edible greens can help you kick your salads up a notch.

DANDELION GREENS

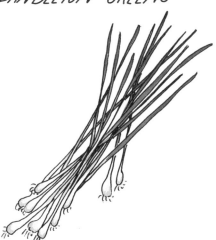

WILD ONION GRASS

you can also eat the bulbs!

WILD RAMPS

find in Oklahoma to the northeastern and southeastern US

ROOTS

CATTAILS

Cleaned, dried cattail roots can be sautéed. They taste similar to artichoke. You can find them throughout the US in freshwater wetlands.

DANDELION

You can make tea made with dried dandelion root to help digestion. You can find them all over the US.

Much of the nutritional and medicinal value of plants is found in their roots.

MARSHMALLOW ROOT

This makes a delicious antibacterial tea that helps ease heartburn and sore throats. Find it in most moist areas like riverbanks.

ROOT OF CHICORY

Ground dried root of chicory can be
added to ground coffee for a rich and
bold taste. Find it along roadsides
and in untamed areas.

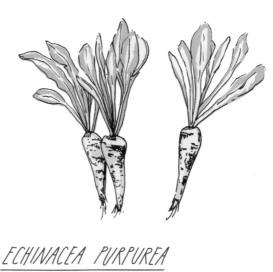

ECHINACEA PURPUREA

There are more than two hundred medicines derived from
Echinacea purpurea root extract, all designed to strengthen the
immune system. The purple coneflowers, leaves, and roots are
the primary ingredient in echinacea immune-boosting teas.
It is found on dry prairies and in open wooded areas.

ANATOMY OF A
MUSHROOM

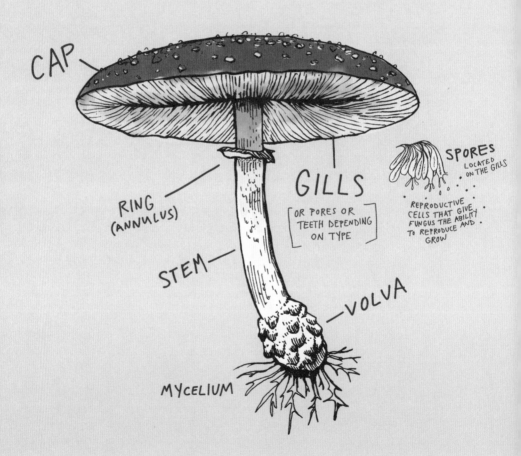

CAP

GILLS

OR PORES OR
TEETH DEPENDING
ON TYPE

SPORES
LOCATED
ON THE GILLS

REPRODUCTIVE
CELLS THAT GIVE
FUNGUS THE ABILITY
TO REPRODUCE AND
GROW

RING
(ANNULUS)

STEM

VOLVA

MYCELIUM

SOME EDIBLE MUSHROOMS
CATEGORIZED BY SPORE DISPERSAL STRUCTURE AND COLOR OF SPORE PRINT

REMINDER! Never eat a mushroom without positive identification. Consult authoritative references and make a spore print to confirm the species (see page 54).

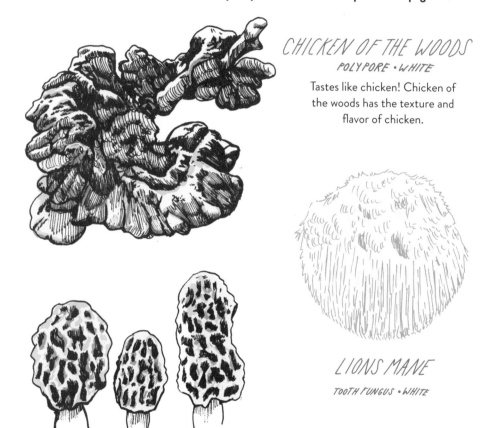

CHICKEN OF THE WOODS
POLYPORE • WHITE

Tastes like chicken! Chicken of the woods has the texture and flavor of chicken.

LIONS MANE
TOOTH FUNGUS • WHITE

MOREL
MOREL GROUP • CREAM TO LIGHT YELLOW

Morels are the foragers' gold. They are very hard to find, but they are in season for months. They begin to pop up when the ground temperature is around fifty degrees and will grow until the average daytime temperature reaches eighty degrees. Depending on where you live, they can be found in any season based on your local climate.

MORE EDIBLE MUSHROOMS

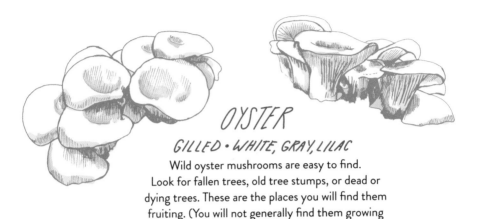

OYSTER
GILLED • WHITE, GRAY, LILAC
Wild oyster mushrooms are easy to find.
Look for fallen trees, old tree stumps, or dead or
dying trees. These are the places you will find them
fruiting. (You will not generally find them growing
right out of the ground.)

CAULIFLOWER / RUFFLES
CORAL AND CAULIFLOWER GROUP • WHITE

DEER OR FAWN
GILLED • BROWNISH TO SALMON PINK

OLD MAN OF THE WOODS
BOLETE • DARK BROWN TO BLACK

Old man of the woods is a bolete mushroom. Instead of gills, it has pores underneath the cap that disperse their spores for reproduction. Old man of the woods are easily identifiable by their dark, crusty, and scaly appearance. When cooked they have an earthy flavor, and—beware—everything you cook with them will turn black.

Chanterelles, while meaty and delicious, can easily be mistaken for false chanterelles, which can be toxic. Chanterelles have forked ridges (not true gills) that are light in color and feel rubbery to the touch. They also have a savory smell with fruity overtones, and when cut down the stem reveal white flesh with a pale middle in the cap. False chanterelles have forked orange gills that can be separated, and when cut down the stem they still reveal an orange center.

CHANTERELLE
CHANTERELLE GROUP • PINKISH YELLOW

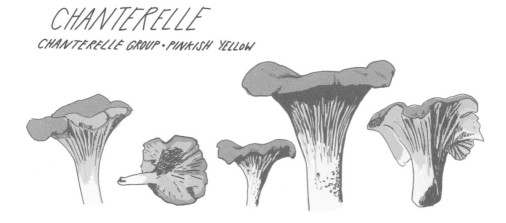

ACTION: MAKE A SPORE PRINT

Another mushroom identification method is to make a spore print. Many mushroom guide books will list the spore color as one of the most effective forms of identification. Plus, it's fun to see what pattern your mushroom creates . . . or the unexpected color it may produce!

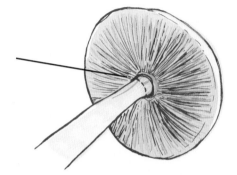

1. Pick two of the same variety of mushroom.

2. Cut or pull the stems from the cap of the mushrooms.

3. Place the cap gill- or pore-side down. Put a drop of water on the top of the cap to help the mushroom release its spores. Place one cap onto a piece of white paper and the other cap onto a piece of dark paper. (If the spores are dark, they will show up well on the white paper and if the spores are light, they will show up well on dark paper.)

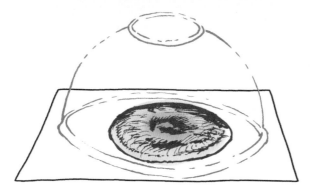

4. Cover the cap and paper with a bowl and leave undisturbed for four to twenty-four hours. Keep them at room temperature. (Don't be tempted to remove the cap early—give the spores time to release.)

5. Remove the caps and admire the pattern they created!

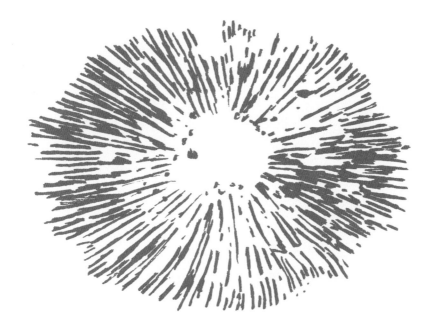

"WHIP' POOR-WILL"

NATURE'S MUSIC IS NEVER OVER;
HER SILENCES ARE PAUSES,
NOT CONCLUSIONS.

-MARY WEBB, PRECIOUS BANE

CHAPTER 4
LISTEN UP, Y'ALL

Step outdoors and listen to the symphony. The sounds of nature demonstrate the creativity and intelligence of the natural world. Nature's music influenced our ancestors' communication and continues to inspire us today. Sounds of the outdoors act as alerts, calming forces, and a form of healing. Take in the rhythms, hear the call and response, follow the little melodies and relax in their presence. Hear how the leaves respond to the wind, the water reacts in the creek flowing over the rocks. Listen to birds communicate and how sometimes they are simply singing to express their contentment.

CHITTER-CHITTER

CHIMNEY SWIFTS

THE SONGS OF SONGBIRDS

Songbirds like warblers, thrushes, and sparrows make up almost half of the world's 10,000 bird species. If you hear an elaborate birdsong, it is most likely a male bird exercising his pipes to attract a potential mate.

HOUSE SPARROW

CHIR-TWEE-CHIR-TWEE WOO

EE-OOH-LAY-EE CHK-CHK-CHK (FLUTELIKE)

WOOD THRUSH

CHEW-CHEW-CHEW CHUG-CHUG-CHUG TITITIT (KINDA LIKE R2D2)

NIGHTINGALE

NASHVILLE WARBLER

TWEE-TWEE-TWEE TU-TU-TU

Sit for a while and you'll begin to notice the ways songbirds use rhythmic variations, intervals, and combinations of notes similar to elements in musical compositions. Did you know that Wolfgang Amadeus Mozart met a starling in a shop that sang the theme from his "Piano Concerto No. 17 in G Major"? Songbirds also transpose motifs into different keys, follow the same musical scales of modern music, and tend to sing in canon.

NORTHERN CARDINAL

Move over Herbie Hancock—the northern cardinal can chromatically run through more notes than are on a grand piano in just a tenth of a second!

PUREET- PUREET-
CHEER -CHEER
WOO- WOO-WOO

BALTIMORE ORIOLE

BER-BE-DU
BER-BE-DU
BER-BE-DU

Actively listening to birdsong is thought to improve our mood and enhance mental alertness. A primary school in Liverpool conducted an experiment of playing birdsong to schoolchildren during their lunchtime and found that students who listened to it were more attentive after lunch than those who didn't. According to a study published in *Scientific Reports*, people exposed to birdsong and natural soundscapes had less depression and anxiety than those exposed to the sounds of traffic and other urban noise.

HAACK-HAACK
HAACK

REDHEADED WOODPECKER

CHER-CHU-CHER-ACK

EASTERN BLUEBIRD

THE SONGS OF BIRDS OF PREY

Birds of prey and birds you find near the shore use their voices to communicate everything from courting to danger and defense.

WHO COOKS FOR YOU? WHO COOKS FOR YOU?

CHIRP CHIRP-CHIRP CHIRP-CHIRP WHII SYLL

BARRED OWL

Barred owls have a distinct spring courting call of eight to nine musical notes, historically described as "Who cooks for you? Who cooks for you?" This call carries well through the woods and is easy to imitate. During courtship, when pairs decide to mate they voice rowdy chortles, hoots, caws, and gurgling growls to affirm their desire for each other.

OSPREY

MISSISSIPPI KITE

TWE-TUUUUU TWE-TUUUUU

CAW-CAW-CAW CAW-CAW

AMERICAN CROW

THE SONGS OF SHORE BIRDS

CHORTLE-A-DEEEEEE

Red-winged blackbirds are found in fresh and saltwater marshes as well as in dry meadows.

RED-WINGED BLACKBIRD

RRR-AAAACK
RRR-AAAACK

CANADA GOOSE

AAAACCCKK ACK-ACK
ACK-ACK

CALIFORNIA GULL

RAACCKK
GROOAACCKK
GOCK

SANDERLING

CHEEP
CHEEP-CHEEP
CHEEP

GREAT BLUE HERON

OTHER SOUNDS IN NATURE

Close by, the cicada song can sound like a buzz saw in a mill, but from a distance you can hear melodies, rhythm changes, and crescendos and the drop. On the day he received an honorary degree from Princeton University, Bob Dylan was inspired to write "Day of the Locusts" after hearing the buzz of a majestic cicada choir in the distance. (Even though cicadas are not locusts.)

CHIRRPBUUZZZ
CHIRP-BUZZ

CICADA

ZZEEEZZEEEEZ

HOUSEFLY

The buzzing sound we hear from bees and houseflies is made by the beating of their wings.

The pitch changes as the pace of their wings changes.

BLACK CRICKET

This little guy will wake you up chirping from his hiding place.

CHIRP
CHIRP
CHIRP

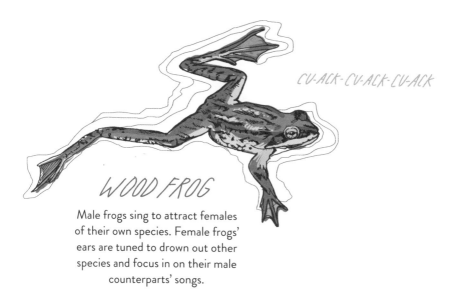

CU-ACK-CU-ACK-CU-ACK

WOOD FROG

Male frogs sing to attract females of their own species. Female frogs' ears are tuned to drown out other species and focus in on their male counterparts' songs.

TSSHHH TSSHHH TSSHHH

TIMBER RATTLESNAKE

What happens when you hear a rattlesnake? If you ever hear a rattlesnake shaking its rattle, slowly move away from the sound. It means back off or else!

Small animals like squirrels and chipmunks use their voices for mating and for warnings about predators.

SEET-BARK   SEET-BARK
(to warn of aerial predator)

*CHIP·CHIP
CHIP·CHIP*

(warning that ground predators are around)

GRAY SQUIRREL

CHIPMUNK

*EEEP
EEEP*

PICA

RACCOONS use more than two hundred different sounds to communicate with each other. They range from growls, purrs, twitters, hisses, and even screams that can sound like a screech owl!

*MAAAOW
MAAOW*

NUTRIA

CHU-CHU-CHU-CHU-CHU
(really fast)

Coyotes rely on their many yips and howls to communicate. You can hear them shift their pitches and modulate between tones. This dynamic vocal range allows coyotes to create howls with personal lilts and trills, so that their pack-mates will instantly recognize them.

COYOTE

WOOAHWOOOOOO

BROWN BAT

KICK·KICK·KICK

Did you know that bats are not really blind? They in fact have excellent sight and use vision to look for food and watch for predators in the daylight. Because of their nocturnal nature, their ears have super hearing power and use echolocation to find their way around in the dark. The sounds they make "echo" off objects to let them know where they are. We can hear some of their chirps, but their sounds are often too high-pitched for humans to hear.

WHEOO-
WHEOO-
WHEOO

WHITE-TAILED DEER make sounds ranging from snorts to clicks: snorts when alarmed (often accompanied with foot stomping), and growls if they are threatened. Bleats are used by fawns when they want attention, and bucks use clicks when they are searching for a mate.

SOUND OF WATER

What does the sound of moving water do to us? Our minds are conditioned to relax when we hear steady, predictable sounds at low to moderate volumes. We hear threats when we hear alarms—a big bang of thunder, phone dings, and the racket of traffic. When we hear natural sounds like a gentle steady rain, a babbling brook, or waves lapping on the shore, our minds hear them as harmonious and dependable—and they naturally calm us.

CASTLE ROCK PARK
MARBLEHEAD, MASSACHUSETTS

The way we hear sound in nature changes with the seasons.
As sound waves move through the atmosphere at different altitudes
and temperatures, they change speed. Sound waves move faster in
warm air and slower in cold air. A bird might sound slightly different when
heard at the base of a mountain than if heard several thousand feet up.

ACTION: *MAKE A SOUND MAP*

Go outside and create a sound map of all that you hear. Use these pages or take a piece of paper or cardboard and write "me" in the middle of the page. For every sound you hear, write it down in the area where you heard it. Write the name of what you hear, draw what made the sound, or write down what it sounded like. You may hear birds chirping above you to the left or a dog barking in the distance behind you to the right.

Slow down, breathe, and listen. You'll discover sounds that will surprise you, and taking time to listen closely will "tune" you into your surroundings.

DRAW YOUR OWN SOUND MAP HERE

SACRED
GEOMETRY

COLUMBINE
WILDFLOWER

IN ALL CHAOS THERE IS A COSMOS,
IN ALL DISORDER A SECRET ORDER.
—CARL JUNG, *THE ARCHETYPES*
AND THE COLLECTIVE UNCONSCIOUS

CHAPTER 5
DISCOVER PATTERNS

"Sacred geometry" is a term that describes the wonderful patterns we see in the world. We interpret these markings as sacred and symbolic ways our world is woven together. They have amazed us for thousands of years. As artists, mathematicians, and philosophers have studied these patterns through the ages, they found that many are not as random as they appear. One underlying explanation is mathematical. Fibonacci numbers, a mathematical sequence in which each number is the sum of the two numbers preceding it, are found in the number of petals in almost all flowers, and in the spiral of a pinecone, a sunflower seed head, and a chambered nautilus shell. These fractal patterns are presented by geometric shapes that repeat at different scales.

Spiral, explosion, packing, meandering, and branching are five of the many patterns that we observe frequently in the natural world. In many cases when we observe these shapes in nature they activate alpha waves in our brains. These waves are a form of neural activity associated with relaxation and meditation. When our eyes take in the unique designs and fractal patterns found in nature, this simple act of observing can have a powerful effect on us. If we take time to muse about these patterns as they present themselves to us, we heighten the effect they can have on us.

FIBONACCI

What determines the number of petals on a flower or the spiraling patterns of Romanesco broccoli? The Fibonacci sequence! The numbers determined by the Fibonacci sequence provide the greatest efficiency for life in a species to continue optimally. Life-forms follow this sequence structure, evolving, ultimately, to the next more efficient iteration of themselves; this process helps them to adapt and live in harmony with their environment.

1, 1, 2, 3, 5, 8, 13, 21... WHAT COMES NEXT?

Mathematically, every number in the sequence is generated by adding together the two previous numbers. This is the simplest example of a recursive sequence— a sequence in which each number is generated using one or more of the previously determined numbers. Romanesco broccoli is a perfect example of a Fibonacci fractal pattern found in nature—each part of the vegetable is a reduced version of the whole.

ROMANESCO
BROCCOLI

GOLDEN RATIO

The Fibonacci sequence is also called the golden ratio (or the divine proportion) and has been used by artists like Salvador Dalí and Leonardo da Vinci. Painters, architects, and photographers have relied on it to find the perfect placement for their subjects and design elements to create balance for our wandering eyes. Composers like Debussy have used the sequence to create melodic progressions of musical keys, allowing the music to flow between sections with a consistent underlying melodic structure.

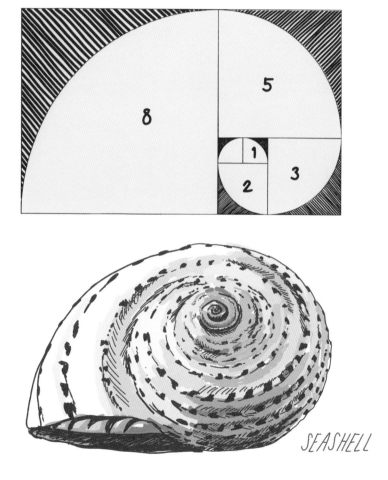

SEASHELL

FIVE DISTINCT PATTERNS YOU CAN FIND IN NATURE

SPIRAL

A spiral pattern can be found in a tiny seashell, a garden snail's shell, a bighorn sheep's horns, a fiddlehead fern, and a galaxy.

SEASHELLS

GARDEN SNAIL

BIGHORN SHEEP

FIDDLEHEAD FERN

GALAXY

EXPLOSION

An explosion pattern is a bursting shape that starts in the center and "explodes" outward.

DANDELION

SWEET
GUM BALL

PINECONE

ORANGE

SNOWFLAKES

PACKING

In a packing pattern, the Fibonacci sequence determines how efficiently things like seeds are packed into fruit. A honeycomb is a great example of how nature uses the Fibonacci sequence to determine the optimal size and shape of the hexagonal waxy cells that best serve the size of their worker bee colonies.

EASTERN PAINTED TURTLE

PINE BARK

HOGNOSE SNAKESKIN

WASP NEST

HONEYCOMB

MEANDERING

The movement of a snake and the crevices in brain coral follow a meandering pattern.

BULLSNAKE

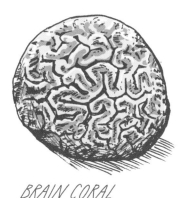

BRAIN CORAL

MANY
A CALM RIVER
BEGINS AS A
TURBULENT WATERFALL,
YET NONE HURTLES AND
FOAMS ALL THE WAY
TO THE SEA.
–MIKHAIL LERMONTOV
A HERO OF OUR TIME

It is impossible to find a river that runs straight for any great length. A river meanders due to sediment erosion that travels downstream and settles where it finds the least resistance.

MAP OF
MEANDERING
U.S. RIVERS

BRANCHING

Branching patterns occur in feathers, leaves, and in the stem of a cauliflower. Lightning branches out when a stream of weakly charged particles moving through the air split from one another. Those particles try to find the path of least resistance through the air, resulting in bolts that look like branches forking their way through the sky.

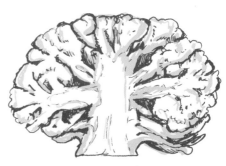

CAULIFLOWER
(CROSS-SECTION)

RED OAK LEAF

SNOWY
EGRET
FEATHER

LIGHTNING

MIGRATION PATTERN

Another kind of pattern found in nature is the behavior of bird migration. Though not as visual as the pattern seen in a flower, migration is a pattern where birds fly to other areas in the world in search of food, for reproduction, and for better conditions. Canada geese use a flying V pattern to share the burden of the flock on their journey and even out the effort required from the whole flock on their journey. The bird in front creates a slipstream that allows the rest of the birds to conserve energy. One side of the V is typically longer than the other. As crosswinds change, one side has to work harder, so birds will switch their alignment from time to time to bear less of the brunt of the crosswinds.

CANADA GEESE

CANADA GEESE MIGRATORY PATTERN

REFLECTION *SOUND VIBRATION*

Another place we can see Fibonacci patterns is in sound vibration. Over the last few centuries, curious musicians and scientists have studied wave phenomena and how patterns can visually manifest. Substances like sand are spread on a flat metal plate and the plate is then connected to sound vibration. The vibration moves the sand particles and it creates different shapes depending on the specific tone. As the frequency increases in pitch, the pattern increases in complexity.

In 1967, the Swiss physician, artist, and musician Hans Jenny published the book *Cymatics: The Study of Wave Phenomena*. His experiments documented the effects of sound vibration on liquids, powders, and pastes. He invented a tonoscope, a simple flat piece of metal that is activated by the sound vibrations from one's voice or music. He was able to produce and document visual patterns that were created from specific sounds like vowels and from recordings of Mozart and Bach. Jenny is credited for naming the study cymatics, but he was not the first who studied visual patterns created by sound vibrations. *The Encyclopedia of Religion* shares that more than a thousand years ago, African tribes placed sand on vibrating drums to predict the future. Leonardo da Vinci and Galileo both observed and wrote about this phenomena. In the late eighteenth century, the German physicist and musician Ernst Chladni created the "Chladni figures." By drawing a violin bow across the edge of a flat piece of metal with sand scattered on top, the resonant vibrations moved the sand into different visual patterns. Mary Waller in the mid-1900s studied the Chladni figures and created mathematical equations to describe the phenomena.

Presently, scientists like Dr. John Beaulieu (who wrote the book *Music and Sound in the Healing Arts*) are studying to determine how sound vibrations physically affect the body and if they can heal.

Dr. Jenny encourages us to "look at the whole and you will come to new understandings. Let these cymatic experiments inspire your imagination to deeper insights into the universal principles of nature."

PATTERN OF SAND CREATED BY DIFFERENT VIBRATION FREQUENCIES ON A STEEL PLATE

YOU ARE THE SKY.
EVERYTHING ELSE—
IT'S JUST THE WEATHER.
—PEMA CHÖDRÖN

CHAPTER 6

LOOK UP!

As terrestrial creatures, humans don't spend much time looking up. We have to keep an eye on the ground ahead to keep from stumbling! But taking time to look up is crucial to appreciating our place in the universe. When the world seems overwhelming, looking up to the sky and allowing it to rinse our eyes and minds can give us serenity and a sense of proportion. Our emotions are like the weather, ever changing and sometimes unpredictable, but like the sky above the clouds, our lives can hold it all and ride the changing winds. Stormy or serene, it all comes and goes, and looking beyond the weather, we know there is a beautiful blue sky beckoning.

CLOUD TYPES

CIRROSTRATUS

very thin, consisting of ice crystals, can visually create a moon halo at night and "milky sun" during the day

CIRRUS

feathery, weather is fair right now, but a change is coming

20,000 ft
(above ground level)

ALTOSTRATUS

often signify a warm front is coming along with rain or snow

ALTOCUMULUS

rows, patches, or layers of globular masses, occasional showers possible

6,500 ft

NIMBOSTRATUS

dark gray at the base, bringing rain but not thunder and lightning

STRATOCUMULUS

layer of white and gray puffs, usually threaten rain more than produce rain

STRATUS

stable clouds, featureless, hazy, sometimes foggy

CUMULUS

fluffy, popcorn-shaped with flat bottoms, fair weather

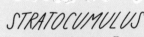

CIRROCUMULUS
white and patchy in sheets, usually short-lived

CUMULONIMBUS
thunderheads, produce rain, severe weather, lightning, thunder, tornadoes

CUMULUS CLOUDS

look light and fluffy, but they are actually very
heavy. A fair-weather cumulus cloud can weigh
more than a million pounds! A cumulus cloud can
grow into a cumulonimbus cloud, which can
be packed with billions, sometimes trillions,
of pounds of water, resulting in rain.

FORMATION OF A TORNADO

Tornadoes are born of rotating thunderstorms called supercells.
These powerful systems can also produce hailstorms.
When warm, humid air rises from the ground and cold air, rain,
and hail drop from the clouds above, a swirling funnel of warm air
gets sucked up into the clouds. As the funnel grows longer and
stretches to the ground, it becomes a tornado.

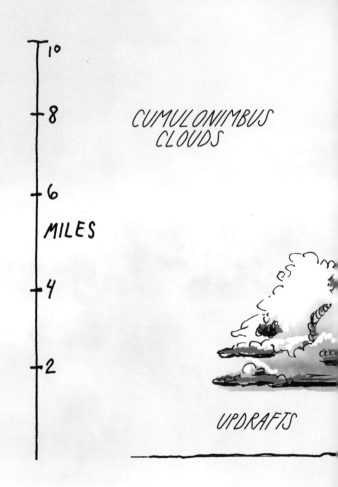

10

8

6

MILES

4

2

CUMULONIMBUS
CLOUDS

UPDRAFTS

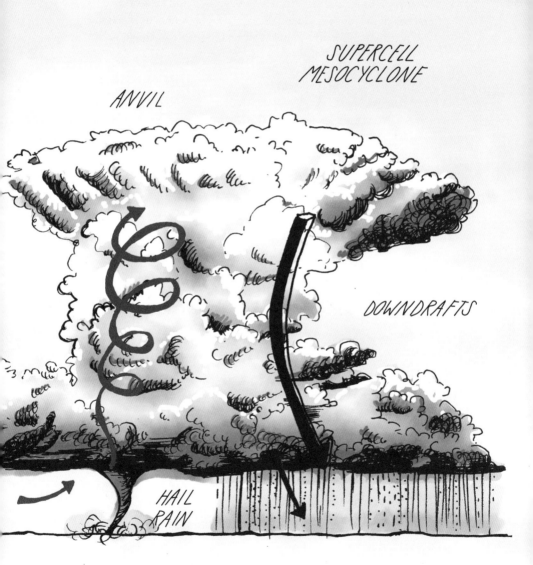

SUPERCELL
MESOCYCLONE

ANVIL

DOWNDRAFTS

HAIL
RAIN

FORMATION OF A RAINBOW

A rainbow is a spectrum of light produced when sunlight shines through raindrops at a particular angle. The rays of light are then reflected by the back of the droplet. A rainbow can only be seen by an observer positioned forty-two degrees from the light source. That explains how that sneaky pot of gold keeps moving on us when we (or the sun) change our distance and angle to the phenomena.

SUNLIGHT

42°

40°

SUNLIGHT

WATER
DROPLET

CONSTELLATIONS

SUMMER IN THE NORTHERN HEMISPHERE

To understand our relationship to the universe, there is nothing more illuminating than looking up into the nighttime sky. To look up at night is to know we are not at the center of the universe. There is a great relief in recognizing our insignificance, especially in moments of distress. We are just a meager yet wonderful speck in the universe. Look at the moon and constellations and relax in your place as the observer— you might find your worries melting away. Some things just are; they are neither good nor bad. Standing beneath the sun, moon, and stars as an observer is a great way to simply be where we are.

Ancient stargazers named constellations for stories rooted in their belief systems. In Greek mythology, Ursa Major was associated with Callisto, a nymph that was turned into a bear by Zeus's chronically jealous wife, Hera. The Yakima people saw the constellation the Romans called Cassiopeia as the stretched and drying skin of a great Elk that was then pulled into the sky. The Skidi Pawnee believed the Corona Borealis was "The Council of Chiefs," and its circular shape is mirrored by the seated position of the elders when they hold council.

PEGASUS

EQUULEUS

CYGNUS

LYRA

DELPHINUS

AQUILA

EAST

OPHIUCHUS

SAGITTARIUS

SCORPIO

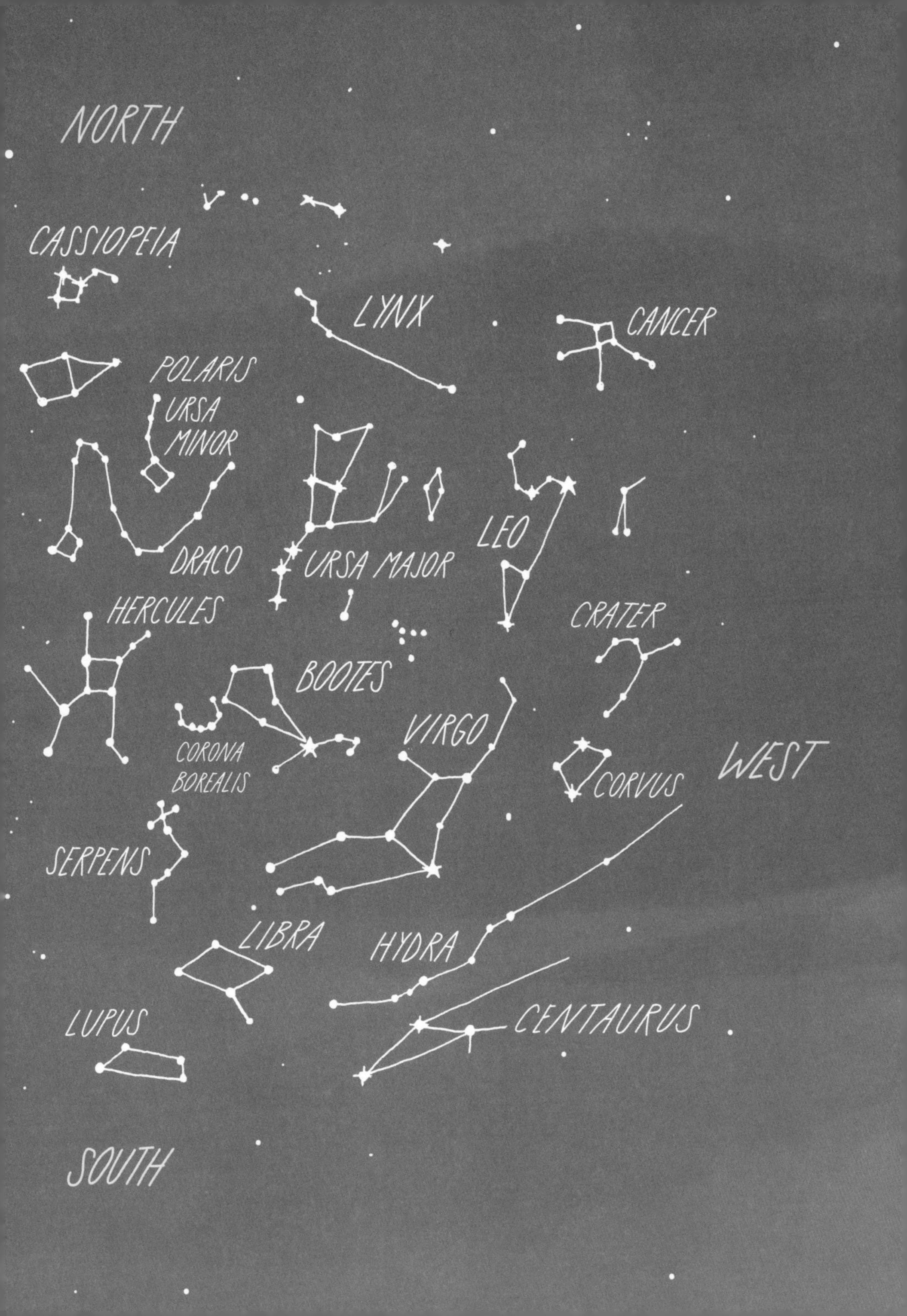
NORTH
CASSIOPEIA
LYNX
CANCER
POLARIS
URSA MINOR
LEO
DRACO
URSA MAJOR
HERCULES
CRATER
BOOTES
VIRGO
CORONA BOREALIS
CORVUS
WEST
SERPENS
LIBRA
HYDRA
CENTAURUS
LUPUS
SOUTH

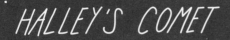

HALLEY'S COMET

A comet is a gaseous, dusty ball of ice that orbits the sun. Halley's Comet is the most famous throughout history. Why? Because it returns every seventy-five or seventy-six years and can be seen with the naked eye. Almost every generation will get a chance to witness this short-period comet. It was last visible in the sky in 1986, and it will be coming back to a nighttime sky near you in 2061.

ACTION: 5·4·3·2·1 TECHNIQUE

We have discussed how we can use our senses to connect with nature in the chapters above. To calm the weather of our mind and simply be—wherever you are—try this mindfulness exercise using all five senses. This is a great centering technique to find some balance when your mind is wandering and distracted, undermining your ability to be in the moment.

5   Go outside, look around, and name five things you can see in nature around you.

4   Focus on four things you can feel, like the breeze in your hair, moisture in the air, or sun on your face.

3   Listen and identify three things you can hear, such as birds chirping or thunder in the distance.

2   Notice two things you can smell. Think fresh-cut grass, the approaching rain.

1   Lastly, consider taste. What can you taste in this moment?

LIST WHAT YOUR SENSES DISCOVER HERE

FULL MOON

THE ONLY LASTING TRUTH IS CHANGE.

-OCTAVIA BUTLER, PARABLE OF THE SOWER

CHAPTER 7

ACCEPT CHANGE

The times are always a-changin'. Heraclitus of Ephesus suggested back in 475 BC that there is only one universal truth about nature: There are no good or bad forces at work, only change. His theory, the unity of opposites, is that opposites are truly the same thing. All is coming and going simultaneously; life and death have equal importance in the cycle of life. Buddhists embrace this idea and suggest that our grasping for one state to be permanent is the root of all suffering. When we accept that change is all there is, we can live in harmony with our constantly changing worlds—both in us and around us.

THE PHASES OF THE MOON

The moon takes 27.3 days to orbit the earth.

There are eight phases of the moon.

SUNLIGHT $\longrightarrow$

Life is full of phases. They all pass.

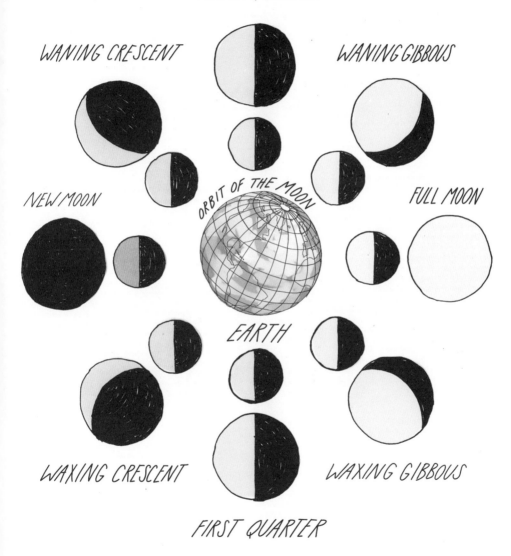

WHAT DO MOON PHASES MEAN TO YOU?

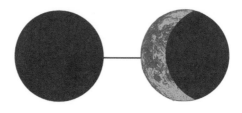

NEW MOON
new beginnings, fresh starts, intention setting, reflection and pause

WAXING CRESCENT
*new energy, putting those intentions in motion,
making plans, exercising body and mind*

FIRST QUARTER
decision making, self-reflection, making commitments

WAXING GIBBOUS
clarity, mindfulness with action, editing and refining intentions

Astrologically speaking, the full moon represents
the balance of yin and yang, while the moon phases are
believed to be a guide for moving forward.

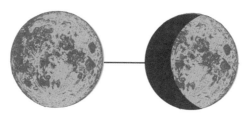

FULL MOON
release, surging power, maximal energy for insight, sealing intentions

WANING GIBBOUS
resilience building, taking stock and evaluation,
gratitude, introspection

THIRD QUARTER
forgiveness, purge and cleanse, letting go of what does not serve you

WANING CRESCENT
surrender, compassion, and self-care

TIDES

All is in flux.
Look to the seas.
The gravitational pull
of the moon is one of the
primary forces causing ocean
tides to ebb and flow. The
moon's gravitational mass
(in astronomy, mass is defined
by how much matter an object
contains, not how much it
weighs) pulls the ocean toward
it during high tides, while
during low tides the earth's
orbit is being slightly tugged
toward the moon. Just as
night and day occur on
opposite sides of the
planet, so do the high
and low tides.

SUN

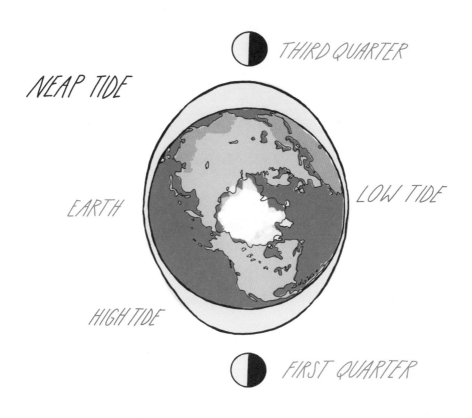

NEAP TIDE

THIRD QUARTER

EARTH

LOW TIDE

HIGH TIDE

FIRST QUARTER

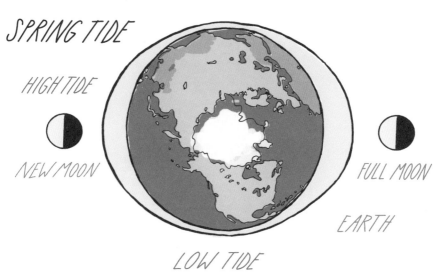

SPRING TIDE

HIGH TIDE

NEW MOON

FULL MOON

EARTH

LOW TIDE

THE SEASONS

Seasons provide us with an unmistakable, never-ending representation of the cycles of life. They serve as a reminder of the impermanence of everything on the planet and in the cosmos. Nothing stays the same. While we might prefer a particular season, none of them is "good" or "bad"; they equally provide what is needed for life to continue with and without us.

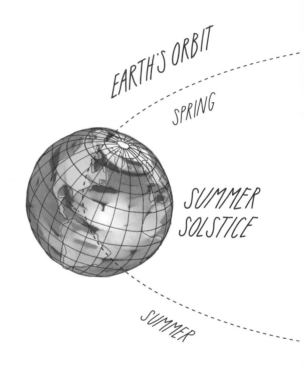

EARTH'S ORBIT

SPRING

SUMMER SOLSTICE

SUMMER

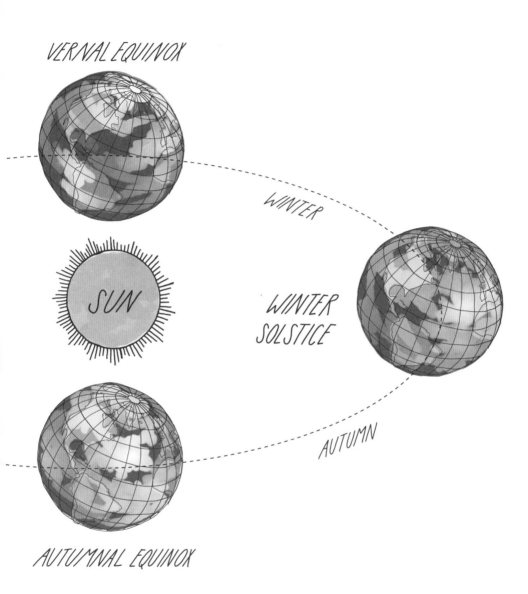

VERNAL EQUINOX

WINTER

SUN

WINTER
SOLSTICE

AUTUMN

AUTUMNAL EQUINOX

ROTTING LOG ECOSYSTEM

GRAY SQUIRREL

DADDY LONG LEGS

AMERICAN BURYING BEETLE

WOODBORING BEETLE

BANANA SLUG

FERNS

That dead tree or rotting log you see decomposing into the ground is teeming with life. In its slow demise to dust and dirt, existing and new life are thriving in and around it. Insect larvae are gestating inside the wood, and animals are part of the little ecosystem. The rotting wood, as it breaks

TURKEY TAIL
SHELF FUNGI

PILEATED
WOODPECKER

WOODLOUSE
SPIDER

MUSHROOMS

LICHEN

LEAVES

CENTIPEDE

BLACK RAT
SNAKE

OYSTER
MUSHROOMS

down, is sending vast amounts of nutrients—like carbon, nitrogen, potassium, and phosphorus—back into the soil, feeding and creating a place for ferns, lichens, and mosses, as well as trees, to continue to thrive. In death it is providing life.

REFLECTION: CHANGE

To reflect on change, we can look to the snake. The adult garter snake sheds its skin two to four times a year. When the process starts, it is said that a snake feels intense anxiety and a sense that death is near—but upon its shedding, the reptile becomes very active in its new skin as if it has a new lease on life. A snake sheds its skin when it has outgrown this outer layer of protection. Shedding also serves to rid the body of parasites, disease, and old wounds that might be attached to the old skin.

Old wounds and ways of thinking that may have served us in the past are hard to shake. When we make a conscious decision to shed old habits in the pursuit of meaningful growth, the loss can feel like a death. When we persevere, dropping outdated modes of being and settling into a new "skin" can lead to a newfound freedom. Embrace change.

GARTER SNAKE
SHEDDING ITS SKIN

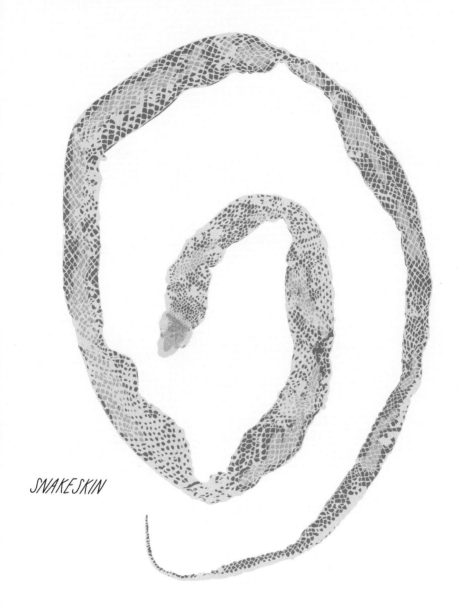

SNAKESKIN

AT THE CENTER OF THE UNIVERSE
DWELLS THE GREAT SPIRIT.
AND THAT CENTER REALLY IS EVERYWHERE.
IT IS WITHIN EACH OF US.

-BLACK ELK

PARTIAL TOPOGRAPHIC MAP OF YELLOWSTONE NATIONAL PARK

CHAPTER 8

YOU ARE HERE

Where are we? Is there any worse feeling than feeling lost? Physically, emotionally, or spiritually? It is difficult to navigate the world when we aren't confident about how to proceed. Just like the great seafaring navigators of ancient lore who discovered that the patterns in the night sky were dependable guides for them to go with confidence and explore uncharted waters and discover new lands, we must find the tools that help us navigate the uncharted waters emotionally and spiritually in our lives. Everyone needs a little awe to inspire courage and a myth to live by.

To better understand where you are physically, look to your natural surroundings. All ancient civilizations, like Native Americans, the Egyptians, the Babylonians, and, of course, Magellan and the great explorers all used a plethora of nature's signs to help them understand their place in time and space, who was close by, and where they might go next. There is great solace in understanding what and whom we share space with on this big blue ball. Being aware of our surroundings instills a confidence that allows us to feel connected and present with all that is around us and in a mindful way we can begin to better accept our time and place in the world.

ANIMAL TRACKS

You are not alone. Learning to identify animal tracks is a fundamental outdoor skill. It also helps you gain awareness of where you are alongside the animals around you in nature. Since ancient times, humans have used animal tracks to find food, avoid dangerous predators, and connect spiritually with the land they live on. Look for a shift in the consistency of the animal's tracks. For example, a deer prefers to walk instead of run to save energy. So if you see a set of four deer tracks followed by an open space, you know the deer started to gallop. If a deer was galloping it was in an emotional state, and it was probably spooked by a predator or spooked by you!

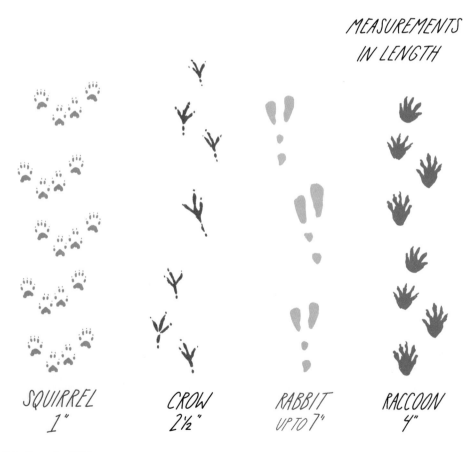

MEASUREMENTS
IN LENGTH

SQUIRREL
1"

CROW
2½"

RABBIT
UP TO 7"

RACCOON
4"

RED FOX
2"

WHITE-TAILED
DEER
3½"

MOUNTAIN
LION
4"

BLACK BEAR
FRONT 4½"
BACK 7"

SUN

Can you find direction by looking at plants? Trees reflect the sun's arc in their growth patterns. In the Northern Hemisphere, the southern side of a tree will appear lusher and thicker than the northern side because the sun spends most of its time in the southern part of the sky. Notice which side moss and lichen grow on trees and rocks. They will grow oriented to the north.

NORTH FACING

MOSS

LICHEN

YOUNG WHITE OAK TREE

SOUTH FACING

PINE TREE

In the southwestern US, a barrel cactus will usually grow slanted toward the south.

BARREL CACTUS

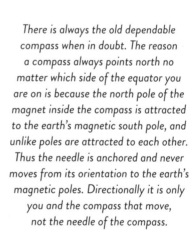

There is always the old dependable compass when in doubt. The reason a compass always points north no matter which side of the equator you are on is because the north pole of the magnet inside the compass is attracted to the earth's magnetic south pole, and unlike poles are attracted to each other. Thus the needle is anchored and never moves from its orientation to the earth's magnetic poles. Directionally it is only you and the compass that move, not the needle of the compass.

COMPASS

The most accessible tool for establishing your bearings
is observing the sunrise and sunset. The morning sun rises
in the east and the afternoon sun sets in the west.
(If they don't, you have entered another dimension.)

SUNRISE

EAST

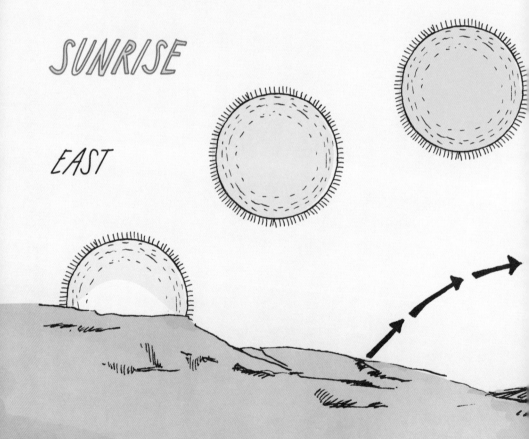

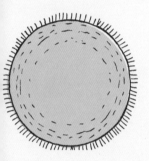

SUNSET

WEST

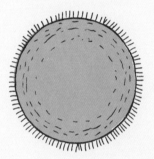

SOLAR SYSTEM

EARTH - THIRD ROCK FROM THE SUN-

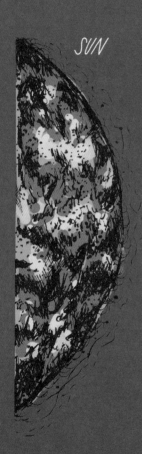

SUN

YOU
ARE
HERE

MERCURY   VENUS   EARTH   MARS

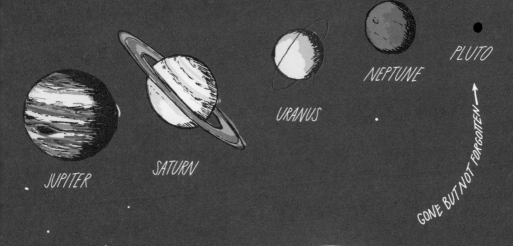

JUPITER

SATURN

URANUS

NEPTUNE

PLUTO

GONE BUT NOT FORGOTTEN→

Our solar system is located in the Milky Way galaxy. There are more than 100 billion solar systems in our galaxy. The sun is over 300,000 times the size of the earth. The earth is over 3 million times larger than a human. Take a second, put your phone down, close the computer, and remember you are not the center of the universe.

URSA MAJOR

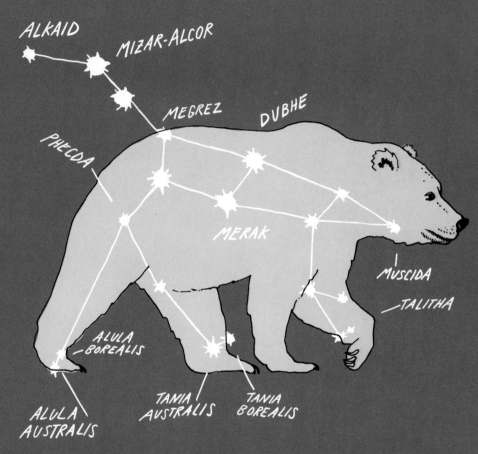

ALKAID

MIZAR-ALCOR

MEGREZ

DUBHE

PHECDA

MERAK

MUSCIDA

TALITHA

ALULA BOREALIS

ALULA AUSTRALIS

TANIA AUSTRALIS

TANIA BOREALIS

Ursa Major is the third-largest constellation in the Northern Hemisphere. The Iroquois tribe called Ursa Major the Great Bear. Many cultures followed the movement of this major constellation and others throughout the year to help them determine when to seed, plant, and reap harvests, as well as to perform religious rites and ceremonies.

THE BIG DIPPER

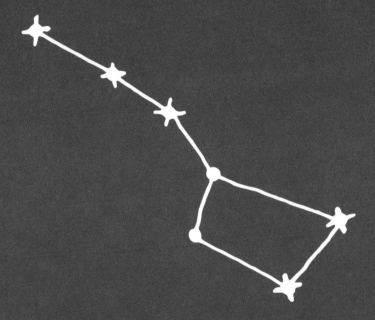

The seven brightest stars create the Big Dipper, the commonly referenced shape or asterism in Ursa Major. Of the seven stars, only six can typically be detected by the naked eye. In ancient Ireland it was known as the Plough. The great seafaring navigators of ancient Polynesia called this constellation Na Hiku, which means seven, referencing the seven stars. The great Polynesian navigators often followed the procession of stars to find their direction on the sea. Up until emancipation, escaped formerly enslaved African American people in the South knew the Big Dipper as the "drinking gourd." By locating it in relation to the North Star, it helped guide them north to freedom.

ACTION: FIND THE NORTH STAR
(SEEN HERE IN THE SPRING SKY)

Finding the North Star (Polaris) is easy on a clear night. Of course, you have to be in the Northern Hemisphere! First, find the Big Dipper. The two bright stars on the end of the Dipper's "cup" align with the North Star, which is the tip of the handle on the Little Dipper.

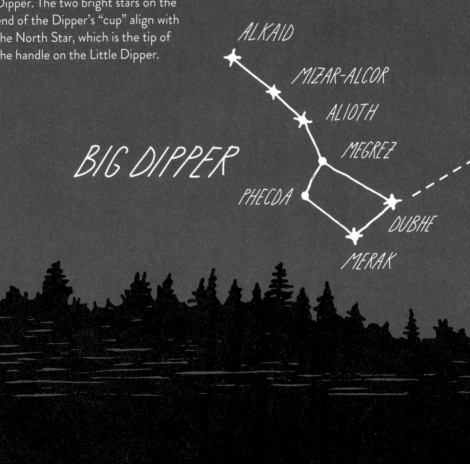

ALKAID

MIZAR-ALCOR

ALIOTH

MEGREZ

BIG DIPPER

PHECDA

DUBHE

MERAK

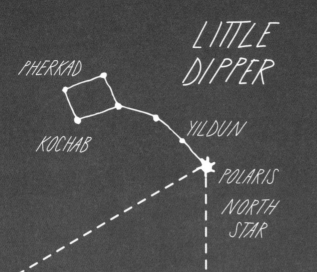

LITTLE DIPPER

PHERKAD

KOCHAB

YILDUN

POLARIS

NORTH STAR

If you are facing the North Star, you are facing north. The North Star is always aligned with the North Pole. While it does rotate ever so slightly in an elliptical pattern, it never moves enough to not be considered due north. (There is no equivalent star that aligns with the South Pole.)

Now identify what is your "old reliable" go-to for centering yourself and being present. What is your spiritual "North Star"? Is it prayer, meditation, a walk in the woods, a personal mythology all your own, a conversation with a loved one, a deep breath? What helps remind you that you aren't lost, a place where you can always return and know you are right where you are supposed to be?

DENALI

HIGHEST MOUNTAIN PEAK IN NORTH AMERICA

DENALI NATIONAL PARK, ALASKA

ADOPT THE PACE OF NATURE.
HER SECRET IS PATIENCE.

-RALPH WALDO EMERSON, *ESSAYS, FIRST SERIES*

CHAPTER 9

TRACE TIME

Time can pass as slowly as a glacier, or as quickly as the blink of an eye. Nowhere is this more evident than in nature. Change in the outdoors is both incremental and dramatic. Almost everything in the natural world takes patience and time to become what it needs to be, but then sometimes it happens in an instant. There is no greater teacher of history than the mountains we hike, the rivers we swim, the great plains that stretch out before us, and that lucky old sun we spin around. Mother Earth was here long before we were and will remain long after we are gone. To truly understand the nature of time, look no further than the earth's landscape as it tells the most epic tale of all: the amazing history of our fair planet.

INTERPLAY OF THE SUN, EARTH, AND MOON

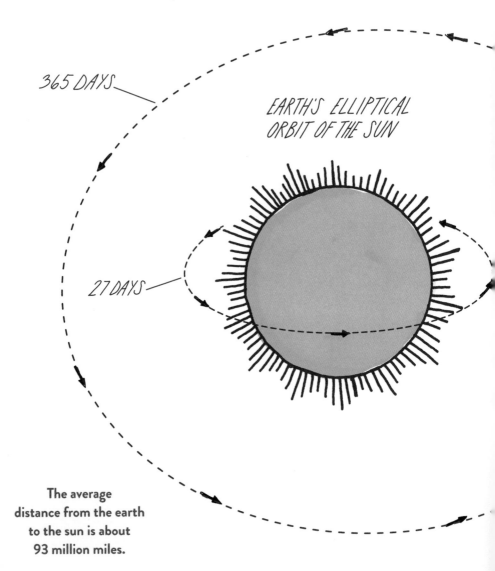

365 DAYS

EARTH'S ELLIPTICAL ORBIT OF THE SUN

27 DAYS

The average distance from the earth to the sun is about 93 million miles.

Time as we know it is an illusion. We can only experience it based on how it relates to the earth's orbit around the sun and the gravitational field at play in our lives. Einstein said, "People like us who believe in physics know that the distinction between past, present, and future is only a stubbornly persistent illusion."

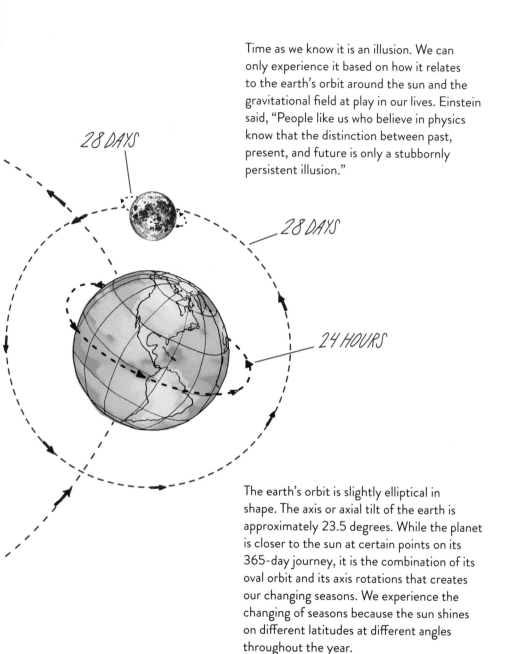

28 DAYS

28 DAYS

24 HOURS

The earth's orbit is slightly elliptical in shape. The axis or axial tilt of the earth is approximately 23.5 degrees. While the planet is closer to the sun at certain points on its 365-day journey, it is the combination of its oval orbit and its axis rotations that creates our changing seasons. We experience the changing of seasons because the sun shines on different latitudes at different angles throughout the year.

MINERALS

Minerals are inorganic solids that are naturally occurring. They were never alive, like plants or animals. They consist of a combination of chemical elements. They are formed over millions of years by intense heat and pressure, through the evaporation of mineral-rich liquids, and from cooling lava deep inside the earth. We use minerals in many aspects of our lives. Quartz is used to make the oscillators in watches, computers, and other electronics. Feldspar is used in glass and ceramic production as a flux, which lowers the melting temperature when firing. This helps clay or glass to harden and become impermeable. Muscovite splits into sheets and has been used as a substitute for glass. In flake form it adds a pearlescent sheen to ceramic glazes. It is also a good insulator and is used in fireproofing materials.

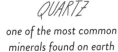

QUARTZ
*one of the most common
minerals found on earth*

AUGITE
*found throughout the
world and has been
found in meteorites!*

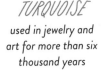

TURQUOISE
*used in jewelry and
art for more than six
thousand years*

FELDSPAR
*the most abundant
mineral on earth*

SPINEL

a gemstone found in metamorphic rocks, it can be red, lavender, green brown, violet, or black

MUSCOVITE

the most common mica

HALITE

commonly known as rock salt

FOSSILS

Petrified fossils form when minerals replace the structure of an organism. This process, called permineralization, occurs when groundwater solutions saturate the remains of buried plants or animals. Most petrified fossils form from quartz minerals, calcite, or iron compounds. The clues of prehistoric life are found in rock formations. Fossilized life-forms give us clues to extinct species that might have never been imagined without their like-nesses being preserved in sedimentary layers of rocks. We can begin to date their time on earth depending on the layer of rock we find them in. It also gives us clues as to what these species might have evolved into so that we might better understand them today.

TYPES OF ROCKS

Rocks take time to form. Like millions of years of time. We see rocks being used every day, in building materials, ceramic dinnerware, kitchen countertops, electronics, and even pencil leads.

SEDIMENTARY rocks are formed by the accumulation of minerals and other organic sediment on the earth's surface that are deposited in layers, followed by cementation, forming a structure known as bedding. The Law of Superposition is fundamental to how we determine age and understand the history of the planet. The major principle is that within a sequence of layers of sedimentary rock, the oldest layers are on the bottom and get progressively younger as they progress to the top.

CONGLOMERATE
clastic sedimentary

DIATOMITE
organic sedimentary

FLINT
chemical sedimentary

IGNEOUS rocks, also known as magmatic rock, are formed through the cooling solidification of magma or lava. Characteristically, igneous rock is not found in a bed like sedimentary rocks; it lacks fossils and rounded grains and is made up entirely of crystals that give it a coarse-grained texture. How fast the magma cools will determine if the rock is created within weeks or millions of years. Extrusive igneous rocks are created when magma cools quickly. Intrusive igneous rocks are created when magma is trapped inside the earth and cools very slowly.

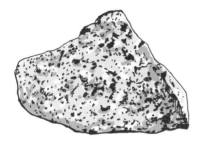

GRANITE
intrusive igneous

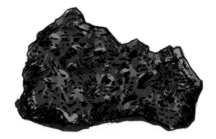

SCORIA
extrusive igneous

METAMORPHIC rocks are rocks that were once igneous or sedimentary. They have been changed (metamorphosed) as a result of intense heat or pressure within the earth's crust. They are crystalline and usually have a "squashed" or banded texture. It can take millions of years to create a metamorphic rock, but exactly how long depends on conditions.

SCHIST
foliated metamorphic

LAPIS LAZULI
non-foliated metamorphic

ANCIENT COURSES:
MISSISSIPPI RIVER MEANDER BELT

Time flows like a river, altering its course for a better path. The mighty Mississippi River has changed its course many times over the last 10,000 years, with gravity being the strongest factor in determining these course changes. When sediment deposits made by the Mississippi become high and flat, the river then finds the path of least resistance to the Gulf of Mexico, hence changing its course. In the 1940s, Harold Fisk created fifteen maps that present an artistic and spectacular historical view of the lower Mississippi changing course over the centuries, from Cape Girardeau, Missouri, to Donaldsonville, Louisiana.

Baton Rouge, Louisiana, to Geismar, Louisiana.
Based on Harold N. Fisk's maps, 1944, plate 22-15.
Each color depicts a different course of the river in history.

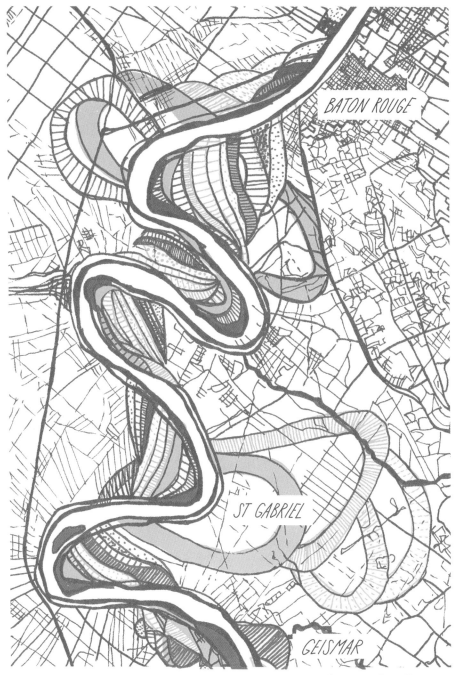

BATON ROUGE

ST GABRIEL

GEISMAR

Wind and water are the great landscape architects of today. Flash floods, rivers, and streams patiently erode rock over decades; the minerals the water carries act like an abrasive, slowly scouring away layer upon layer of soil and rock. The high winds of the desert have a similar effect, sending tiny rock particles whizzing through the air. These particles shape rocks, hills, dunes, and canyons.

LOWER FALLS
YELLOWSTONE
NATIONAL PARK,
WYOMING

GREAT SAND DUNES
NATIONAL PARK,
COLORADO

PEDESTAL ROCKS
SCENIC AREA,
ARKANSAS

TUNNEL ARCH
ARCHES NATIONAL PARK, UTAH

CONTINENTAL PLATE CONVERGENCE

Mountains are formed when two tectonic plates collide. When two plates have a similar density and weight, neither one will sink under the other. Instead, they force each other upward and fold in on top of each other, forming mountain ranges. The longer the collision lasts, the higher the mountains.

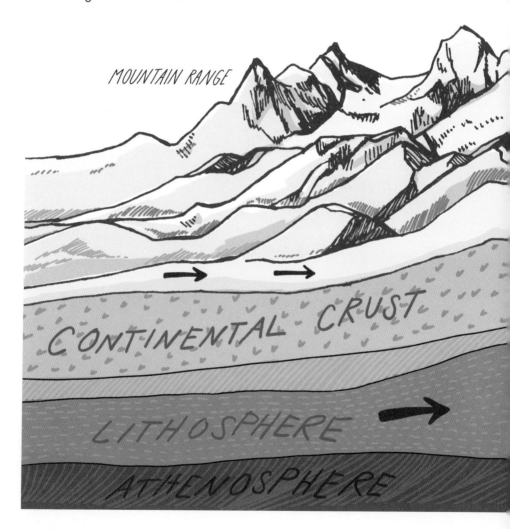

MOUNTAIN RANGE

CONTINENTAL CRUST

LITHOSPHERE

ATHENOSPHERE

Generally, mountains are classified as either young or old. Young mountains like the Rockies and Himalayas were created only a few dozen million years ago. They tend to have steep dramatic slopes and high, pointed peaks like Denali in Alaska or Grand Teton in Wyoming. Old mountains, like the Smoky Mountains, have rounded peaks and domes made gentler by hundreds of millions of years of erosion, including interacting with ancient oceans.

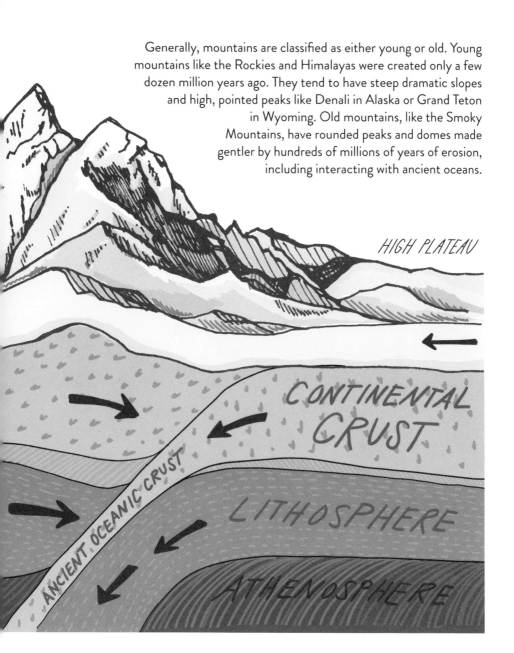

HIGH PLATEAU

CONTINENTAL CRUST

ANCIENT OCEANIC CRUST

LITHOSPHERE

ATHENOSPHERE

ACTION: WRITE A HAIKU

Haikus are often inspired by nature and time. They are a great way to elevate and document a moment or a feeling. A Haiku is a three-line style of poem created by Japanese poets beginning in the seventeenth century. It follows a 5-7-5 syllable structure and is read in one breath to vibrate its impact.

Use something you see outside today as inspiration—anything. Write a haiku. It doesn't have to rhyme.

For instance:

First line, 5 syllables

Tennessee in Spring

Second line, 7 syllables

Violet and deep blue blooms

Third line, 5 syllables

Sway for me, they do

I bet you can do better than that . . .

WRITE YOUR HAIKU HERE

IF WE SURRENDERED TO EARTH'S INTELLIGENCE, WE COULD RISE UP ROOTED LIKE TREES.

-RAINER MARIA RILKE, *RILKE'S BOOK OF HOURS: LOVE POEMS TO GOD*

CHAPTER 10

REJUVENATE

Researchers suggest that an environment devoid of nature acts as a discord in our lives, which can have an undesirable impact on our health and overall quality of life.

Something as simple as having a better view of trees from our workplace or adding a few more houseplants to our inside places can add to our sense of well-being. There is a reason why when we are stressed out, a simple walk outside in a natural environment can help us refocus and relax. It is harder and harder to break away from our trance of screens, but we should as much as possible. On a grander scale, spending more time on the lake, in the woods, or at the park offers the time and place to reconnect with ourselves and the world around us. Biophilia studies all suggest nature is the place where we recharge and heal from stress, hardship, and traumas. The word "biophilia" comes from the Greek "philia" meaning "love of," and literally means love of living things. We need to allow ourselves this time outside to rejuvenate our mind, body, and spirit.

We always have time for the little pauses. Being mindful and engaging our senses on little walks through our garden or taking a slow walk with our dogs in the park can really matter. Take time to be in the moment. All life and nature is changing. Seasons come, seasons go. Hard times come, hard times go. Good times come, good times go. Our planet supports, heals, and nurtures us emotionally as well as physically through all the changes in our lives. Make spending time outdoors part of your routine.

CIRRUS CLOUDS
20,000 FT ABOVE GROUND LEVEL

Nature always gives us a place to go when we are feeling stuck or unwell. We are not just what we think; our bodies are sacred places too. So often we forget to scan our bodies and senses and feel the incredible aliveness that is happening in us. By reconnecting with our sensory awareness, we can truly be in our bodies and not three feet outside ourselves in thought. Once we get centered by our senses in a specific time and place, we can experience well all that lives around us. Listen to the music of the birds, notice the breeze through the grass and trees, smell the rain in the air or the leaves decaying, touch the bark on your favorite tree, taste

the honeysuckle growing wild in your backyard, and of course, forage for yummy mushrooms. This is the mindfulness that we can all benefit from, in our mind, body, and spirit. The simple act of stepping into your backyard or taking a long walk in the woods provides a time and place to connect with a living and loving presence—our beautiful planet—in real time. Our heart rate slows, our stress levels reduce, our brain orients to a calm alertness of our surroundings, and our senses come alive— helping us experience aliveness more abundantly.

Nature is a place where we can come to terms with our true essence. When we intentionally seek out the wonders of nature, we experience life more fully, and these experiences always invite us to be more present and appreciate the joie de vivre.

Life's great lessons are all around us, reminding us to surrender, adapt, let go, evolve, live, and—no matter how old you are—be amazed.

We can observe the ancient animals and plants that still walk the earth. These species have let go of old ways, evolved, and adapted, and they continue to be here for thousands, even millions of years.

HORSETAIL

species 300 million years old

BRISTLECONE PINE

in the southeastern California White Mountains—oldest tree in existence today at 5,000 years old

ALLIGATOR

150 million years old

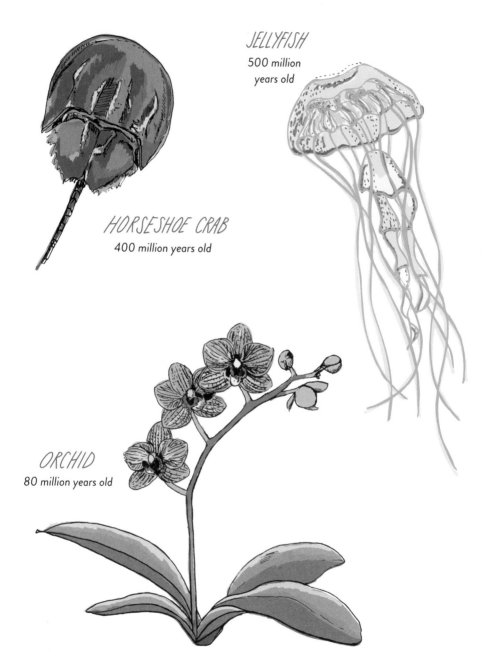

JELLYFISH

500 million
years old

HORSESHOE CRAB

400 million years old

ORCHID

80 million years old

Seek out nature wherever you are. Even on your travels, make sure you carve out time to experience the landscape and environment of the new places you visit. It will not only give you a respite from a packed itinerary but also allow you to fully immerse yourself in the life of the area.

We all experience a strong and ancient pull to the grand places in nature. If you have ever been to the Grand Canyon, Yellowstone, or the Redwoods, you know how when you leave, the place sticks with you and continues to tug you back both spiritually and physically. Reconnect to that ancient pull. Go to the mountains, the ocean, the rivers, the deserts, and the forests of this wonderful world. You will never regret it.

REDWOOD FOREST, CALIFORNIA

CASTLE GEYSER
YELLOWSTONE
NATIONAL PARK,
WYOMING

It is no mystery that the great landscape painters throughout history understood the ancient pull of nature. Artists like Robert S. Duncanson, Thomas Moran, and Utagawa Hiroshige all instinctively knew that we crave the connection to nature that society's progress invariably moves us away from. We place these artworks in our museums and in our homes as places to reflect on the earth's magnificence. Consciously or unconsciously, they remind us of the ties that bind us to the landscapes we live in and tread upon.

Places of worship aren't sacred places simply because clergy or your shaman tells you so; they are because you attune yourself to the spirit there. And it is because of how you feel when you are there. There are sacred places everywhere. Nature is the Great Cathedral for us to find our happy. These canyons, forests, coastlines, and backyards for that matter are the places that many of us nature lovers depend on for our peace of mind—the places outside that when we go there, we sense our wonderful place in this grand harmonious scheme of life on earth. Your sacred place might be simply a park bench, a favorite tree that you stop by on your walk and give a little love tap—any place where you are comfortable enough to allow your mind to quiet and your senses to heighten. It might be a special place in your garden where you always sense your aliveness in the moment.

Find your sacred place in nature. When you alone determine where your spot is, know that it is sacred. Why? Because you said so. Practice your sensory awareness and breath awareness wherever you go. Be there, and be joyful.

CATHEDRAL ARCH, SAN JUAN COUNTY, UTAH

ACTION: A HIKING MEDITATION

While walking in nature to your self-described sacred place, consider a walking meditation. Walking has always been an activity that helps declutter the mind. As you begin your hike, allow your mind to do its planning and problem-solving. But as you gain your rhythm and get a little sweat on your neck, practice coming back to the moment; your breathing, your feet touching the ground . . . and relax.

First, notice your mind. Is it still busy? Notice your heart. Has it found its tempo as you move? Notice the body. Are there any spots where you are holding tension or discomfort? Give them some attention and consciously soften those places. Allow yourself to accept what is going on in your mind, heart, and body. Some days are more distracting than others. Name it. Sometimes naming it gives you a pause to move past it if it is a negative feeling. Are you feeling anxious, angry, or joyful? Allow it to be what it is and release it if you can. If it's joy, embrace the blessing. The mind will always try to pull you back to thinking. When you notice your thinking instead of experiencing it, bring attention to your breath and feel your presence in the moment.

Try a breathing technique. With your mouth closed, breathe in through your nose for a slow count of six. Exhale through your mouth for a slow count of six. Do this for a couple of minutes, and notice the calming effect. Your heart rate will come down, your blood pressure will drop, more oxygen will be absorbed and more CO_2 retained, all increasing the calming effect. After a few minutes, breathe through your nose into those places that are tight or uncomfortable—spots that you might have identified earlier—and then breathe out the tension. Relax into those spots, softening them on the exhale.

Get out of your head and back into your body. Your sensory awareness will be calm and heightened after you practice breathing. Gently listen to the patter of your feet and what they are treading on. Feel your shoes, your feet in your boots, the skeletal structure performing beautifully in your feet. Allow your eyes to notice the light of the day, how it looks through the clouds or trees. Notice the subtle movements of critters scurrying, birds darting among the trees, the wind through the grasses. Gently touch a tree as you walk by. As your breath steadily softens, smell what is in the air and taste it if you can. As your mind inevitably tugs you back to anticipating and planning the day, go back to your breathing technique. Notice your mind settling again and your heart opening up to experiencing your walk more fully.

When you get to your spot, ideally the halfway point on your hike, pause and maybe sit on the ground or on a downed log for a while. Gently put your hand on your heart and feel your aliveness. Let your senses bounce around your environment. Try to cultivate that sense of gratitude, knowing that it is good to be alive and experience such moments of self-care and love. Feel how the mind, body, and heart have benefitted from your walk. Take this sense of well-being as you walk back to your destination. Remind yourself to carry the feeling back into your busy world knowing that the natural world is always a place for you to escape and heal.

Epilogue

Rekindling a relationship with the natural world and getting out of the "built" world will likely take you by surprise. The benefits of spending time in nature, especially in wild places, have been proven by study after study, and yet still there is this great disconnect in civilization that we can live apart from nature. It's not our fault. This devolving, as it were, has been going on for at least eighty generations. And while poets, scientists, doctors, psychologists, and philosophers alike have all pointed time and time again to the fact that our overall well-being is connected to spending time in nature as well as conserving it, our illusion of our separateness persists.

The science is outpacing any concept of this book. There is so much to learn and it all points to both our physical and psychological need to be in the wild. Rubbing some dirt on it is likely more prophetic than the ol' ball coach ever knew. Our minds need nature. Humans prefer objects naturally existing in nature that are complicated, that are growing and changing and sufficiently unpredictable enough to be interesting. People who get bored in nature are just not paying attention. When nature is not a mindful presence in our lives, the chance of experiencing awe is dramatically less than when we curate time outdoors. Awe and that sense of wonder increase happiness and lower stress levels. The benefits are likely immeasurable.

In the modern world of screens and dings, commutes, noise pollution, bills, the perceived and real hostilities that our fellow humans are waging against each other, our unconscious anxiety about giving up on the planet totally bombards our sympathetic nervous system, which stimulates the body's response to danger and puts us in this perpetual state of fight or flight.

On the other hand, the parasympathetic nervous system, the system that helps us relax and recover from stress, is more likely to be activated when we take a walk in the woods or a park. Simply taking a ten-minute microbreak by going outside to breathe the fresh air and look at the sky can improve your concentration considerably. It is more important than ever to take breaks in nature.

We have had Mother Nature on the run for some time. Now we need to start living more mindfully with her, by understanding that interconnectedness and being awed by the wonders right outside our door. When we are in the wild, the myth that we are the takers and overseers of the earth begins to fall apart. The fact that we are merely an equal part of everything in nature can only help foster the concept of conservation and stop this trance of needing to subdue or dominate nature.

Go find your tempo and rhythm outside, curate time there, find your sacred place, and be comforted by the fact that this big blue ball and the universe that holds it are much more clever, complex, and wild than our arrested brains can imagine at the moment. Spend more time "out there," choose to touch the earth, learn about science, and find bliss and awe in the most unexpected places. It will happen just by being there. So, go on, put your boots on and get outside, you won't regret it.

CLARKSON POTTER/PUBLISHERS
An imprint of the Crown Publishing Group
A division of Penguin Random House LLC
clarksonpotter.com

Library of Congress Cataloging-in-Publication Data is on file with the publisher.

ISBN 978-0-593-57775-2

Ebook ISBN 978-0-593-57776-9

Printed in China

Art and hand lettering by Kathryn Hunter

Editor: Angelin Adams | Editorial assistant: Darian Keels
Designer: Nicole Block
Production editor: Serena Wang
Production manager: Luisa Francavilla
Prepress color manager: Zoe Tokushige
Compositor: Nick Patton
Copyeditor: Alison Kerr Miller | Proofreaders: Erica Rose and Katy Miller
Publicist: Felix Cruz | Marketer: Chloe Aryeh

10 9 8 7 6 5 4 3 2 1

First Edition

Kathryn Hunter is a printmaker and mixed media artist in Baton Rouge, Louisiana. Since 2003, she has operated Blackbird Letterpress, a small printshop that designs, prints, and assembles handmade notebooks, quirky animal-shaped greeting cards, and products featuring inspiring women. She exhibits her fine artwork in galleries across the United States. Her art incorporates animals as characters in the folktale tradition, commenting on false prophets, social justice, America's freedom, and the erosion of our environment.

Bo Hunter is a poet, writer, and musician who recently finished his first novel. He is a graduate of the University of Alabama with a BA in English and political science. He currently lives in Nashville, Tennessee, and is the brother of Kathryn.